WHAT

THEY

DIDN'T

TEACH

YOU IN

FILM

SCHOOL

WHAT THEY DIDN'T TEACH YOU IN FILM SCHOOL

What you actually need to know to succeed in the industry

Miguel Parga

ilex

An Hachette UK Company
www.hachette.co.uk

First published in the United Kingdom
in 2019 by Ilex, an imprint of
Octopus Publishing Group Ltd
Carmelite House
50 Victoria Embankment
London EC4Y 0DZ
www.octopusbooks.co.uk
www.octopusbooksusa.com

Design and Layout copyright ©
Octopus Publishing Group Ltd 2019
Text and Illustrations copyright
© Miguel Parga 2019
Cover design by Luke Bird

Distributed in the US by
Hachette Book Group
1290 Avenue of the Americas
4th and 5th Floors
New York, NY 10104

Distributed in Canada by
Canadian Manda Group
664 Annette St.
Toronto, Ontario, Canada M6S 2C8

Publisher: Alison Starling
Commissioner: Frank Gallaugher
Managing Editor: Rachel Silverlight
Editor: Jenny Dye
Art Director: Ben Gardiner
Designer: e-Digital Design Ltd
Production Assistant: Serena Savini

ISBN 978-1-78157-717-2

A CIP catalogue record for this book
is available from the British Library.

Printed and bound in China

10 9 8 7 6 5 4 3 2 1

Additional picture credits:
55 © Julia Basques and
Giovanni Fabietti 2019;
66, 112, 118, 127, 138, 155, 164, 210,
214 © Gabriela Azuaje 2019;
25, 36, 144: Director of Photography:
Nick Snow (NYFA production);
27 and 96: DP: Emmanuel Trousse
(NYFA production);
31, 61, 78, 199: DP: Nicolás Peribonio
(NYFA production);
47: DP: Brian Dilg (NYFA production)
56, 88, 143: DP: Brian Dilg;
81, 128, 133, 145: DP: Giovanni Fabietti
104: DP: Luis Alarcón (NYFA
production);
115 and 213: DP: Giovanni Fabietti;
160: Drawings by Miguel Parga, DP:
Brian Dilg (NYFA production);
161: Drawings by Miguel Parga, DP:
Brian Dilg;
The photographs on pages 66, 112, 118,
127, 138, 155, 157, 164, 210, 214 were
taken at the New York Film Academy.
iStock: 10 and 71 bjones27;
13 CasarsaGuru;
Unsplash: 8 and 44 Chris Murray; 20
Alexis Brown; 40 Becca Tapert; 49,
139 and 190 Jakob Owens; 68 Nik
Macmillan; 107 Sharegrid; 123 Wahid
Khene; 124 Noom Peerapong; 148
Alexey Ruban; 152 and 168 Kyle Loftus;
182 Feliperizo; 187 Sterling Davis;
188 Jose Lebron; 192 John Schnobrich;
200 Jake Hills; 204 Ryo Yoshitaki;
207 Krists Luhaers; 208 Mattias Diesel;
218 Steven van;
The Metropolitan Museum of Art,
New York: 54. Bequest of Benjamin
Altman, 1913 (CC0 1.0)

"It is wonderful to create."

Akira Kurosawa

contents

INTRODUCTION

Here's a little secret for you: Most people who teach at film school have no idea what they're doing. It's normal. Artists generally have no idea how they do what they do, let alone how to teach it to somebody else. It's part of the nature of art that there's an element of mystery to the way it happens. Many artists foster this element—they revel in it. To teach something is to break it down into its moving components, to deconstruct it, and then to organize it into digestible parts that others can understand and absorb. Most artists don't want to do this, as it would kill the magic.

Here's another alarming fact I've discovered about film education. A large number of the people who teach at film schools have never been paid to make a movie, direct a commercial, write a screenplay, or work on television. Some of them just went through school, got their degrees, maybe directed a few shorts in the process. But that's about it. They're there because they need a job, just like you will when you graduate.

I suspect that most art forms were better learned in an apprenticeship setting, where you spent years observing a master at work, absorbing little bits of information as you went along. Then the master taught you one element of the art form, and you did that for a few years. Then they taught you another aspect of it, and so on, until eventually you were the one doing the thing and the master retired. It was obviously a slow process but a lot of art forms used to do it, and it worked.

That method, however, is not practical, as it's time-consuming and doesn't generate revenue, so it has largely disappeared now that education has become a business. Today's graduates have to go to work right away in order to pay the enormous debt they have incurred while getting their education. Some, especially arts graduates, go right back into the school system and start to teach.

The film business is mega-competitive, and getting a job right out of school is hard. That's something to consider as you make the massive decision whether to invest all the money it takes to go through film school. Most of the people who teach there wish they were somewhere else, doing what they had set out to do. Some of them may be excellent teachers, but it's important to know what you're paying for. Do some research—know what you're getting into.

The aim of some institutions has become not just to stay afloat but to thrive in a very competitive market, which means they have to be able to offer a product that appears better than the competition, even if it is not actually better. And if one of their competitors cuts corners, they may have to do the same or risk being outsold. When choosing a film school, you need to watch out for these pitfalls.

This book is about what you need to know as you go through the process, because ultimately your education is in *your* hands. Learn to get what you want. Unless you are proactive in this, people will only give you what *they* want. You're entering a super-competitive business. Don't wait for somebody to recognize your talent and hand over the keys to the kingdom. People don't get discovered by the poolside in Hollywood (or if they do, it won't be for anything worthwhile). Waiting is death.

Thousands of people graduate from film school every year. They're all competing for a finite number of jobs, in an already oversaturated market. Once you graduate, you'll be competing with your professors for the same jobs.

A few years back, unemployment in the Screen Actors Guild was at around 90 percent. And that was counting only actors who at some point had gotten a job with the Guild, not those who had joined but had never worked, or actors who had worked but weren't members to begin with. If we took those numbers into consideration, the percentage would be more like 98 percent. Yet people continue to flood into film schools, in the hope of someday becoming part of the business. Why go into a career that's so competitive?

I think that it's because a hunger for stories is part of our DNA. To survive in prehistoric times, humans had to compete for food and shelter with other creatures, but humans had an advantage—their brains could absorb, interpret, and apply information better than any other creature. Stories were the first tools of learning that humans had, to try to explain their world. Somebody would get up in front of the fire and tell a story. The audience, sitting in the dark, would learn from the story, and those who were able to learn would survive. What's more, when people traveled, the story traveled with them and others could learn as well, even across vast distances. That's a huge evolutionary advantage.

Today we still have that insatiable appetite for knowledge. Being able to tell stories gives you prestige. People listen; they're entertained; they learn. That's almost a superpower. When you can manufacture what people want, that gives you confidence and poise, not to mention a monetary reward.

Filmmaking is the premier method of storytelling today—or at least the most popular at the moment. That's one reason that more and more people want to do it, despite how competitive it is. Add to that the massive salaries paid to those at the top of the pyramid. The dream exists: "Why not me?"

Those are compelling forces to make somebody want to become a film director despite the odds. Another reason is that it is addictive. Frank Capra said, "Film is a disease...as with heroin, the antidote is more film."

Filmmaking is one of the few endeavors in life that taxes every aspect of who we are. There's the often overwhelming physical challenge of making the film: months of working long hours with limited breaks, often under tough conditions. There's also the mental challenge of solving the ever-changing puzzle of making a movie—it's a constant battle between wanting to do your best and having only limited resources. Plus, of course, there are the things that can and will go wrong on set. You have to continually reinvent the movie as you're making it. You have to think on your feet and you have to adapt.

Finally, there's the emotional aspect of sharing your story with the world, of putting your creation out there for everybody to see and criticize. It's terrifying. Are you good enough? Is what you have to say important? What if it isn't? What if it flops? What if people hate it? Or, worse yet, what if they ignore it?

There are few things in the world that challenge you at so many levels. And because it is so demanding, we are tragically attracted to it. We have to do it—because as human beings we have an ongoing love affair with the impossible. What does the word "impossible" mean anyway? It's all just a human construct. But we enjoy that dichotomy. We enjoy being able to do what's most difficult.

One of my good friends in this industry who is a regular collaborator of mine used to say that film was the only thing that made him feel totally alive. He craved being on set and he suffered depression when he wasn't. That's something they don't tell you—there's a huge down after you finish a project. Your body has been engaged so intensely for the period of the shoot that once you're done, you don't know what to do with yourself.

prepared

I remember when I was working for ABC News there were people there who had been having that reaction for 20 or 30 years. You could see it in their eyes. They were addicted to the adrenaline of being on the air. They lived for that moment when they felt useful and necessary. What human beings crave above all else is a purpose, and film provides that in spades.

So if you've got the fever and you've decided film school is the way to go, then here's the information you'll need to know when you get out. Some of it they'll teach, some of it they won't. Some of it they won't even know you need, but, trust me, you do.

I know—I was once in your position. But I've never held a job that's not related to the arts, and even though I've had my ups and downs, I've loved every moment. You can do the same.

I live for what I do. It's my purpose. I've been in this business for 25 years because it fills a need, because it gets me up and going in the morning, and because I love the face my students make when they learn something new.

If you're going to do this, if you're really going to dedicate your time to film, you have to be prepared to fail—and then to keep going…because there's nothing else in this world you can see yourself doing. That's the type of commitment you need to survive in this business. There will be times when all you're going to want to do is quit. Just shake off that feeling and get to work—this ain't for the faint-hearted.

If you know that this is what you want to do for the rest of your life, then you're going to need knowledge. You'll also need stamina. And, most of all, you're going to need what students want more than anything else in the world: inspiration. Let's get to it.

"There will be times when all you're going to want to do is quit. Just shake off that feeling and get to work—this ain't for the faint-hearted."

ONE

WHAT YOU SHOULD
TAKE AWAY FROM
FILM SCHOOL

So you're going to film school—fantastic. Here are a few things you should make sure you get while you're there.

READING AND WRITING

At film school you'll hear a lot of contradictory advice about writing. It's one of the toughest disciplines to master, and, like many art forms, sometimes those who are doing it have no idea how they do it, even when they are very good at it.

The best-selling author Stephen King, in his book *On Writing*, says, "If you want to be a writer, you must do two things above all others: read a lot and write a lot." That's the secret. If you want to get good at writing scripts, you have to read, *a lot*! And you have to write, *a lot*! There's no way around it. You cannot be a good writer, or a good artist for that matter, if you don't read.

Part of what we do when we write is continue a conversation that other writers have already started. It may be about technique, inspiration, the nature of art, the iniquities of life, suffering, injustice…anything. It doesn't really matter what the focus of your writing will be. What matters is that you know where that conversation is at, so that you can take the next step.

That's never going to happen if you don't read. One of the most common mistakes young writers make is to repeat themes and conversations that have already been covered exhaustively by other writers.

Reading is an intimate conversation with another mind. The writers of the past have left their legacy to you, so you need to take advantage of that and activate your mind to new ideas and modes of thinking.

writers

commitment

I believe a writer should read every day—and especially every night before going to bed, so you prepare yourself for what you'll do the next day, which is write. Get in the habit of taking a book with you everywhere you go. Read in bits and pieces or, if you have the time, take in big chunks at one sitting. How you do it doesn't matter; all that matters is that you read. If you don't, you'll never be a good writer, and good writing is the beginning of the process of making a movie. You can't make a great movie from a mediocre script.

So this is the first commitment you need to make if you're going to become a good filmmaker: Pick up a good script or a good book, and read it.

"I read on the internet," my students tell me, but that doesn't count. The stuff you read online has been designed to be consumed in a very short period of time. Instead of helping your imagination and focus, what it's doing is having the same effect that being on your phone does, which is shortening the amount of time you focus. You need long, immersive reading, to get lost in the story, to stretch the muscles of your imagination.

You should be doing that every day. In his book *On Writing,* Stephen King says he goes through maybe 70–80 books a year. I can't manage that many, but I think I go through at least 30, which is a different book every couple of weeks. You have no time to waste…you're already behind.

Method

First things first: How are stories told? It's simple. Humans tell stories with a beginning, a middle, and an end. This is the way our brains work. Ever since the first written accounts from ancient history, this has been the preferred method for telling tales. There's something that calls to us in stories constructed in this way.

If you deviate from this structure, you may come up with something new and exciting, or you may fail terribly. That's all good and fine. I hope you experiment and find a way to make movies and tell stories nobody has ever come up with before. But I suggest that as an apprentice filmmaker you should first aim to master the most common way to tell stories: with a beginning, a middle, and an end.

Some screenwriting teachers will say to you that there's no set way to tell stories, but that's nonsense. Yes, it's absolutely possible to break from that norm and still tell a great story. Most of the masters of film did just that, and made amazing films as a result. Bergman, Fellini, Kurosawa, Kubrick (to name a few) all did it. But before you start experimenting, you must master the basic method.

Author Note
If you haven't read
Robert McKee's
book *Story: Substance,
Structure, Style,
and the Principles of
Screenwriting*, put it
on your reading list.

Classical Design

Robert McKee, the renowned writing teacher,
calls this preferred structure of having a beginning,
a middle, and an end Classical Design.

Classical Design is how the great majority of television
shows and movies are constructed. It's the bread
and butter of the industry. Learn it, master it, own
it. If you get good at telling stories this way, you will
inevitably entertain. And ultimately that's what people
want: to be entertained. They want to become the
people on the screen, to live vicariously through them.
Learn to give the audience what they want and love.

Components

Here are the components—the nuts and bolts—
of the process of constructing a story.

The dilemma

A good story starts with a dilemma. A dilemma is
a problem with two options, both of them bad. For
example, a mysterious hacker you admire tells you
you're trapped in the Matrix. You can ignore that
information and continue to live your life, or you
can get out and be persecuted by authority. What's
it going to be?

Another example: You're a kid and you miss your dad,
who left you and your family to go and live his own life.
Now an extraterrestrial lands in your backyard, and
you become friends. Do you help him to get home,
even though he's your one true friend? Or do you try
to keep him here, even though it might kill him?

A strong dilemma keeps the audience glued to the screen. It's the one question they spend the movie trying to answer. But coming up with a good one is not easy. Try it—think of a problem that has two possible solutions, both bad. Now you have the beginnings of a script.

One of the things poor writers do is come up with a problem that has two solutions but they're not both bad. Then, because they need the story to keep going, they have the character make the bad decision. This is major cheating and the audience will smell it a mile away. It's like that scene in the horror movie where the girl is in her room, hears scary noises in the attic, and decides to go and have a look.

That's not real, it's a lie. If you construct your story on a lie, it's hard, if not impossible, to come back from that. But if the same girl hears noises in the attic and her baby's up there, you have a dilemma. Now you have an interesting situation. But please, come up with a true dilemma.

Conflict and empathy

Once you have your problem, you will need to make the story move forward, but here are some things to consider first.

First, everything that happens in a movie happens through **conflict**. This is crucial. Your job as a filmmaker is to make the life of your protagonist hell. The harder you make it, the better. Some people might say that it's because we like to watch others suffer, and there's a level of truth to that. We do love a train wreck. But there's also a more technical reason: The audience must feel the emotion of **empathy** toward the protagonist.

Empathy enables you to understand what the person is going through. It is a much stronger emotion than, say, sympathy, because you can feel it toward somebody you don't really like. In the movies, this happens all the time. We feel empathy for characters who under normal circumstances we would despise. Tony Soprano is a great example of this. We empathize with him from episode one of *The Sopranos* even though he's a criminal and a murderer. We even feel empathy toward Hannibal Lecter!

The first tool you have for creating empathy is to make the life of the protagonist hard. As the audience sees them struggling with the iniquities of life, they relate, because ultimately we all feel like the world arrays itself against us. Life conspiring to keep us down is part of the human condition.

As humans, we all know we are swiftly traveling toward our end. It's the great unfair truth of existence, and suffering is a natural reaction to this realization. So we feel a kind of kinship toward a person who's suffering, because we ourselves suffer. It's only human.

So pressure, pressure, pressure! Hardship, hardship, hardship! The more, the better. Then you hit them with a good dilemma, and you're well on your way.

Decision

The scene with the dilemma is called the **inciting incident**. There are many other names for it, like **plot point one**, but I prefer inciting incident. From this point, you have to move the story forward. How do you do it? This is one of the most difficult things to teach. Students seem to get it and then forget it. We all do. I can sometimes trace problems I might be having with a script back to forgetting about this component.

One way to move the story forward is to have the character make a choice. Unsurprisingly, this is known as **decision**, and it is simple—the character makes a choice. You want a protagonist who has an object of desire, which emerges from the first decision, the one they make at the dilemma. After making that first decision, the character continues to try to get what they want.

For example, a guy walks into an ice-cream store. He wants both vanilla and chocolate ice cream. However, he only has enough money for one. Dilemma.

He must make a decision as to what to do, so he reaches into his pants and pulls out a gun—he has decided he's going to rob the place. He demands a cone with both vanilla and chocolate ice cream. "Go ahead…make my day."

When the character makes a choice, it moves the story forward. Now, whenever they make a choice, they have an expectation of what that choice will bring. You must deny them that expectation, and you have to keep denying it, perhaps until the end of the story.

So our ice-cream bandit wants both vanilla and chocolate, and he pulls out a gun to get them. He expects to get them, but you can't allow that. Robert McKee calls this the **gap of expectation**. It must remain open.

Revelation
The second way in which you can move the story forward is revelation. As the ice-cream bandit is looking down the barrel of his loaded gun, he notices something strange about the clerk at the ice-cream store. It turns out that the clerk is a girl who went to grade school with him. His first love. They had kissed once and then he had moved away. They haven't seen each other in 20 years. She recognizes him, too, and after they have said their hellos, the clerk gives your protagonist what he wanted, a cone with both vanilla and chocolate ice cream. That's revelation. You change the circumstances and move the story forward in that way.

Your protagonist is still enjoying his double cone of goodness as the police put him in the cruiser. He and the clerk make gooey eyes at each other as the police take him away. End of movie.

Silly? Maybe, but absolutely Classical Design. If you wanted to continue this story, the characters would have to continue to make choices or you would have to set up a few more revelations. Then the scenes can keep moving forward. You would also have to give the characters a new object of desire. He got his ice cream already, so something new must emerge. Perhaps the second half of the movie centers around her trying to break him out of jail. Then they go on a rampage robbing ice-cream stores. You could title it *The Sugar Cone Bandits*.

revelation

Acts and sequences

Movies, like plays, are divided into **acts**. A feature-length film has a minimum of three acts—a beginning, a middle, and an end—but it can have more. Some movies have five acts, seven, twelve. Each act has a climax, which is a scene with a higher dramatic content that usually signifies the end of the act.

Scenes organize themselves into **sequences**, which are just groups of three or more scenes that have their own mini-climax at the end of the sequence. The ice-cream store robbery is a little sequence that leads to the arrest of your main character. The ending of a sequence usually opens questions that set up the following sequence. Now the ice-cream store clerk is going to figure out how to spring her newfound boyfriend out of jail. When she does, then it opens up the question of how they are going to survive. Well, they decide to go on an ice-cream store robbery rampage, which sets up their being hunted by the police, and so on.

A sequence climax answers the question of its own ending, and the answer sets up the question of the following sequence. The characters continue to make choices, and revelations continue to happen. You may reveal that the detective assigned to the case also knew them in grade school. He used to bully your protagonist.

Sequences add up to form an act with a more dramatic **climax**. Perhaps in your act climax you reveal that the detective also kissed the ice-cream store clerk, creating a wedge between protagonist and new girlfriend. Now the protagonist doesn't know whether he can trust her.

Author Note
For an excellent book
on movie sequences and
how they work, check
out Cherry Potter's
*Screen Language:
From Film Writing
to Film-making.*

Notice how the act climax involves an emotional
escalation. That's usually a good way to up the ante.
Drama in a movie always climbs. You can do it by
making the sequences more and more physically
demanding or you can escalate the emotional and
psychological consequences.

Turning scenes
Scenes must move the story forward, which is called
turning the scene. In Classical Design, and in fact in any
good screenplay, every scene turns. Every scene! Every
scene is either a decision or a revelation.

turning

By telling stories this way, you'll be able to keep the attention of the audience. Movies tend to be extremely complex in terms of the implications, but their plotlines work best when they're simple. This is because of the nature of the medium. In film we tell stories with pictures, and those stories tend to be simple because they're observable.

Think back to the silent movies: Charlie Chaplin running to get on a train is a simple little story line. He's just trying to get on, but he's not fast enough, and he's trying to carry his bags, and he has a dog with him, and all sorts of things can and will go wrong. Why is he getting on that train? Well, that's the complex part. He may be going back home to visit his mother, whom he left when he went off to seek his fortune, but he hasn't found his fortune yet and he has to go home because his mother is sick. This sets up the scene in which they meet again, and that's a very complex one because of all the layers of meaning in it. Yet the plotline is simple. Charlie just wants to get there.

If you learn to use the mechanism of decision and revelation, you'll be way ahead of the competition. One of the recurring mistakes I see in student films year after year is that students don't turn scenes. And let me tell you, if you don't put those choices or revelations in there, no matter how short your film is, even if it's five minutes, it'll be the longest five minutes of your life. I've sat through countless student screenings full of films that don't turn, and I'd rather watch paint dry. Don't forget: You must learn to turn the scene.

plotline

I know, you may be the type of artist who doesn't want to make Hollywood films. You may not want to construct your narrative using Classical Design, but want to discover a new way to tell stories. I applaud you for that and you should find your own way, as all the great filmmakers did. But you still need to start from somewhere, so master the form first. You should have a thorough understanding of how Classical Design works when you get out of film school. Don't let anybody fool you into believing that you don't need to learn this, that stories are malleable, or that movies should be made in a more organic way.

If you want to work in this industry, you'll have to get good at telling stories the Classical way. Most of the work you'll do follows that norm. The ability to tell stories in this fashion is called storytelling talent, which some people possess naturally. When they tell you a story, you are riveted. It is the ability to put scenes in a sequence that keeps the audience wanting more.

The techniques I've outlined here will help you, but you still have to work on your skills. How you present the information is what will make it your own, so practice!

HOLDING YOUR AUDIENCE

Here's a good exercise. Take your sequence of events—your story—and pitch it to somebody in five minutes. Observe their reaction. If they're interested in what happens, that's good. If they can't wait to hear what comes next, that's better. If they seem bored or are doing other things while you're telling the story, that's not good at all. In that case, your story needs work. If you can't hold your audience for five minutes, what makes you think that making it longer is going to make it any better? If it was boring in five minutes, it'll be even more boring in two hours. Don't write your script until your story can hold your audience for at least five minutes. Make that a rule to live by.

Dialogue

This is one of the hardest things to learn. Some teachers believe that you can't learn it, that you either have an ear for dialogue or you don't. There's some truth to that—some people just understand the way others communicate; they understand the rhythms. At any rate, whether you have the gift or not, you can always improve your skills, so here are a few pointers.

Miscommunication

Think of dialogue not as a method of communication but rather as a method of miscommunication. Words are just an approximation of what we feel and want to say. Often in a conversation, one person is talking about one thing, and the other is saying something completely different. They're talking at each other but neither is listening. Then something happens and maybe they connect for a second. At that point they're both listening intently. This lasts maybe a few seconds, and then they're back to not listening, like in the following piece of dialogue:

INT. KITCHEN—MORNING
Frank reads the paper sitting at the table. Gary enters.

> GARY
> If that woman ever…

> FRANK
> Did you see this story about the kids that went missing?

> GARY
> If she ever…

> FRANK
> They wandered through the woods for three days.

> GARY
> Are you listening to me? I think Thelma's cheating on me.

Frank puts the paper down, covers a NOTE on the kitchen table with it, making sure Gary doesn't see.

> FRANK
> You sure?

> GARY
> She thinks I would never notice something like that. She's always underestimated me.

> FRANK
> Well…do you have any idea with whom?

Frank takes the note from under the paper, crumples it, pretends to read the article about the kids again.

> GARY
> She's always underestimated me.

> FRANK
> Three days…that makes no sense.

know

The characters are having separate conversations until something happens. Then they're together for a second, then they go off again.

Notice that there's plenty going on under the lines. Does Frank know about the cheating? Is he involved? We don't know yet. All we know is he's trying to hide whatever's on that note. There is plenty of opportunity for moments when the characters are not saying anything but the camera is on them, which is good.

Subtext
The camera loves subtext. It loves it when the actor has something to say but doesn't say it, and when the actor says something but means something else.

36

The camera cuts through the eyes and lets us know there's something happening inside. That's why what's really happening in the scene happens under the lines. This is the way conversation goes in real life sometimes. Language is only an approximation to communication. Even if we wanted to say everything that's in us, we often can't. We are islands unto ourselves. We can't really tell what's going on inside somebody's mind, and we can never completely communicate to others what's in our own mind.

Humans are aware of this. That's one of the reasons we have art—it's a way to communicate what's inside our minds. I create a painting, or a sculpture, or a film, in the hope that by seeing it and experiencing it you can understand how I feel. That's how aware we are of the imperfections of language. We can't just say it—we have to convey the emotional content in some other way. Stephen King, in his book *On Writing*, calls writing telepathy. All art, in a way, is telepathy.

Give the actors plenty of moments when the characters are not saying anything. A good actor can communicate more with their eyes than they ever can with a piece of dialogue. In movies, the dialogue in the scene often doesn't explicity state the true meaning of the moment. This is to give the actors something to play while they're saying the lines.

Listening

Listen to the way people talk. They don't do it in perfect sentences, but in fragments, trying to figure out what they want to say as they say it. Next time you're at a restaurant, on a train, or in a ticket line, listen to the conversation happening right next to you. Learn the rhythms of speech. Pay attention— you never know when you're going to get a beautiful piece of dialogue.

Author Note
I was once having brunch in East Hampton, New York, and I heard a woman at the table next to me say, "Howard, you're a fat man. You can't wear white." Gold! I've used this, or something similar, in two scripts already. You can't make up stuff like that. It's so perfectly composed, so perfectly charged with humanity.

rethinking

Polishing

Take your time and make sure the script is where it needs to be. This is a hard lesson to learn and follow. We are always so eager to go and shoot. *The New Yorker* magazine featured a cartoon of two cavemen, one of whom is drawing a scene from a hunt on the wall of a cave. The other is heading out of the entrance carrying a bow and saying, "Enough storyboarding. Let's shoot something."

As much as I can identify with that sentiment, I know that problems with the script will only amplify with shooting. A script needs time to cook. You have to write it and rewrite it and rewrite it again. It's a never-ending process of polishing something, right up until the last minute. Writer-directors often have to hire a writer in order to keep polishing as they get closer to principal photography. Stanley Kubrick used to do this, but he also continued to work on the script himself as they shot. There's some famous footage of him typing away on the next day's pages as Jack Nicholson gets ready for a scene they're about to shoot on the set of *The Shining*.

Remember that you make the film at least three times. You write a script, then you shoot it, and finally you cut it together. Any one of those processes can make or break the film. You have to reinvent your narrative each time and adapt it to the problems of every stage of the process. This is good, as it helps you iron out the wrinkles of your narrative. By the time you're done with that movie, you know the material inside out, and you've gotten everything you're ever going to get out of it.

Don't trust your first idea about how to solve a creative problem. Push yourself for another answer— you can almost certainly come up with something better. The discipline of thinking and rethinking is crucial in filmmaking. You can't afford to turn off your brain and cruise. Try to see both sides of a point, and look at each side with equal intensity. Thinking is debating with yourself, so don't get lazy. Embrace the grind—that's what making movies is all about. Become friends with it, as it'll be there throughout your career.

Only when you're certain that your script is ready can you move forward. If something's wrong with the story, it'll only be amplified with the next two stages. Something that was a tiny problem on the page will become a major story flaw by the time you're trying to cut the film together. Fix it now, when it involves only a few keystrokes.

In his book *The War of Art*, the American writer Steven Pressfield talks about how the committed artist "has to love being miserable," because he has "volunteered for hell…dining for the duration on a diet of isolation, rejection, self-doubt, despair, ridicule, contempt, and humiliation." I suggest to you that it is the proper state for a filmmaker as well. So embrace not just the grind but also the misery.

Welcome adversity with open arms. Some of your best ideas will come out of something that goes terribly wrong and you have to rethink. Never stop challenging yourself. The moment you get comfortable, you start getting soft. I love the beginning of *Apocalypse Now* when Willard is in the hotel room and he's thinking, "Every minute I stay in this room, I get weaker. And every minute Charlie squats in the bush, he gets stronger." He's eating his dinner squatting on the floor. That should be you, thinking about how to become a better filmmaker. Remember, your best ideas are just waiting to be birthed in the open fires of struggle.

But what should I read?

This is one of the questions I get asked the most. Pick up a list of the American Film Institute's 100 movies to watch, and read all those scripts. Or take the winners of the Oscars for Best Original Screenplay and for Best Adapted Screenplay from the last 20 years, and read those scripts.

In fact, those are good movies to watch as well. I'm astounded by the number of students who want to be filmmakers but who don't watch films (other than the current superhero fare). Watch as many films as you can, of all varieties: foreign films, old films, indie films, everything. How can you become a good filmmaker if you haven't seen what the masters have done before you? Some of the names you should be aware of are Kurosawa, Fellini, De Sica, Antonioni, Bergman, Goddard, Truffaut, Kubrick, Altman, Wilder, Ford, Hawks, DeMille, Kozlowski, and Leone, to name just a few.

A book every writer needs to read is *The Elements of Style* by William Strunk, Jr, and E B White. There is absolutely no substitute for this book and no better or more concise guide to the craft. If you haven't read it, put this book down now and get your hands on that one. For a suggested reading list of other books, see page 220.

scripts

CAMERA

Here's one of the great things about cameras: Once you learn the basics of one, it makes it a lot easier to learn to use others. And there are always going to be others. A new "it" camera comes out almost every six months.

I'm not going to go into the technical aspects of cameras (you'll get plenty of that in film school). Instead, we'll look at how to use this tool to tell your story, which is what it's all about, after all.

Different shots affect the audience in different ways, so a big tool in communicating the story is to use the right shot at the right time. The fact that the audience is not always aware you're doing so makes what you're trying to say in the movie a lot more powerful. This is one of the superpowers of film. When you change the shot, you're telling the audience something's about to happen, but since they're hopefully immersed in the story, they're not always aware you've done so.

Continuity and the Axis of Action

As filmmakers we are constantly playing tricks. Film is an illusion. We must help the audience suspend their disbelief and get into the story. One of the tools we use for this purpose is **continuity**, which in films refers to continuity of time and space. It is a trick we play on the audience, making them believe that what they're looking at is happening in real time.

powerful

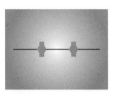

When two actors are in a room, an imaginary line runs through the center of them, dividing the room in two. It is called the **Axis of Action** or the **180-degree line**.

Once you start shooting the scene from one side of the axis of action, the camera can move 180 degrees on this side but it may not cross that line. This is called the **180-degree rule**, and you'll learn a lot about it at film school, as it's one of the basic rules of continuity. The 180-degree rule can be broken, but if you're a beginner, stick to the rule.

By shooting in this way, the character standing on the left side of the screen remains on the left, and the one on the right remains on the right, which helps the audience orient themselves. Because we shoot in a three-dimensional world but the audience experiences the film through the two-dimensional screen, the audience associates a side of the room with a side of the screen.

When you learn filmmaking, you're really learning a foreign language, because film language is the ability to communicate with the audience using the shot rather than words. And you can use the 180-degree rule to communicate with the audience, because the closer you get to the Axis of Action and to the subject, the more dramatic the shot becomes.

If you're looking at a **wide two shot** (two people shot with a wide lens, to include some of their surroundings) that is 90 degrees from the Axis of Action, this is a great shot to establish a room and to show some physical activity. But as you're only seeing the human face in profile and at quite a distance, the shot is not particularly dramatic, unless there's some cool action going on, so it's a good shot to start the scene.

As the scene progresses, moving the camera closer and closer to the Axis of Action and to the subject will tell the audience that the dramatic moment in the scene is about to happen.

Changing the shot tells the story without the audience being aware of it. The most dramatic shot is almost on the Axis of Action, in extreme close-up. Think of that shot of Hannibal Lecter as he's talking to Clarice in *The Silence of the Lambs*. His face is huge on the screen, and right up close and personal with yours.

Moving shots

Camera moves fall into two categories: motivated and unmotivated. A **motivated camera move** is when the camera follows a moving subject. Think about the long tracking shot of Henry and Karen walking into the Copacabana nightclub in *Goodfellas*. The camera follows them from the moment Henry gives the keys of his car to a valet, going through the back door and some hallways, through the kitchen and reception, all the way to the front of the club, where the couple get a bottle of champagne from some of Henry's gangster friends. The beautiful shot accomplishes exactly what director Martin Scorsese wanted. It shows Henry interacting with his environment, and it captures the hustle and bustle of the place, the excitement of being at the Copacabana in New York.

It's a daring shot, because what the character is doing is daring and larger than life. Scorsese's choice of shot helps tell the story of this character's life. This is a highpoint in Henry's career as a gangster. Later, as the character descends into the hell of having to sell drugs to survive, the camerawork becomes more staccato, with fast cuts and moves. Who can forget the amazing, paranoid hell of the helicopter scene at the end of the movie?

The camerawork is there to help you. Changing the shot is not meant to be done at random just because you have gotten bored with what you were looking at. Where you put the camera, what's in front of it, and when you change the shot all tell us something about what's going on. Camera movement puts us in a particular mood as well.

An **unmotivated camera move** is when the camera moves but it's not following a moving subject. This has two purposes:

- ■ It builds tension, because the audience knows that the camera doesn't move unless something's about to happen. Think about a slow moving shot, down a dark hallway in a horror movie—you know something's about to come out of one of those rooms.
- ■ It delineates internal movement. Imagine a character sitting by the window; we're looking at a medium shot of the actor. The character opens a letter and reads a terrible piece of news; the camera pushes forward fast all the way to a close-up. We know now that this character has read something in that letter that caused them some distress. The camera move mimics the internal movement of the character.

movement

The speed of the camera in these cases is important. Imagine the same scene but now when the character reads the letter, you move the camera in at a much slower pace. This time, we know that what they read has affected them deeply, but perhaps it wasn't as shocking as the previous example.

The audience is smart. They are well versed in the language of film. They don't need to have studied the art form to understand. Remember, they've been going to the movies since they were kids. They may not know the technicalities of it but they get it intuitively.

Composition

There's a "dance" that happens in movies involving the camera, the subject, and the environment. Don't disregard any of these three factors, because this "dance" is essential for the creation of an emotional response in the audience. By "dance" I mean a relationship between these elements, but I think the word dance describes it better, since it involves elements of a special relationship, shape, and rhythm.

Some environments demand a certain type of shooting, so go on location before your shoot. Take pictures and feel your way through the space. Let the architecture affect the way you look at the place. See how you feel when you're there, and try to transfer this feeling to the audience in the way you shoot.

When you arrange your actors in front of the lens, do it in a way that's pleasing to the eye, using your own judgment—if it looks good to you, then trust your eye.

You'll learn at film school about the composition technique known as the **rule of thirds**, but it basically works like this. Draw two equally spaced horizontal lines across the screen, dividing it into three equal parts. Do the same for two vertical lines. What you end up with is a tick-tack-toe board with nine boxes.

The eye is drawn to the areas where the lines intersect, so place important elements of the frame in these areas. When doing a long shot, place the figures there. When doing a close-up, place the eyes of the subject there.

Remember that the audience experiences the film through the screen, which is a two-dimensional medium, so strive to convey the three-dimensionality of the world with this technique. Always keep in mind what's in your foreground, middle ground, and background. I find it particularly effective when the foreground and background move in different directions. This happens with moving shots if the composition is correct, and it always gives me a sense of space that is otherwise lacking when looking at the screen.

The shot changes because you cut, or because you move the camera, or because the actors move. Don't be afraid to change the distance between the actors and the camera, or the relationship of the camera to the space. Make the shots dynamic. A shot could start as a long shot, then the actor gets nearer and it becomes a close-up. Next, the actor crosses the room to meet another person—the camera pans with him, and the shot becomes a two shot.

CASE STUDY: *MANHATTAN*

There's a scene in Woody Allen's movie *Manhattan* that takes place in a museum planetarium. It consists of nine shots, almost all of them static, as the characters move through the planetarium. Often the shot starts by looking at something we don't recognize, then the characters move into the light and the true composition of the shot is revealed. When we don't know exactly what we're looking at, this **ambiguous space** is used to unsettle and confuse the audience. The characters are going through an disturbed period in their lives, and the composition echoes the emotional content of the story. That scene in the planetarium is a lesson in composition and lighting.

Woody Allen is the master of this. His shots move with the actors and change composition constantly, which keeps things dynamic. Also, he keeps the cutting to a minimum, to call attention to what the characters are saying—and in Woody Allen movies, conversations are extremely important.

The best way to improve your skill at composition is going to the museum. Study the paintings of the masters—they all had a keen eye for composition and lighting. You really can't do better in terms of improving your camerawork than walking through the halls of a good museum, especially to see the Old Masters. If you don't have a museum near your home, then go online. Type Old Masters into your Google bar and see what you get.

Right: Rembrandt Harmenszoon van Rijn *Self-Portrait*, 1660 Oil on canvas

Lighting

I once went to a science museum where in one exhibit there was a large metal pipe with a hole in it. You were supposed to stick your hand in the hole, so I did. Even though the pipe was dark inside, when I put my hand in it my hand was lit. There was light traveling from one end of the pipe to the other. The light never touched the surface and so it looked like it was dark inside.

This is one of the major principles of film lighting. You want to see the light hitting the subject, but you don't necessarily want to see where the light would have landed if the subject weren't there. In other words, the audience sees only the shadows you want them to see.

You'll study plenty of lighting setups at film school, starting with basic **three-point lighting**, which has a **key light** shining on the subject, a **fill light**, and a **back light**. One thing to keep in mind is the angle of the key light, which can create entirely different moods. Check out the different angles of the key light shown above and what they evoke.

Always be aware of the shadows you create. The greater the difference you produce between places of light and places of shadow, the more contrast you have in your shot. Heavy contrast lets the audience know that there's something dramatic going on.

Affinity is when you have less of a difference between places of shadow and light. The more affinity there is, the less shadow you get. The more contrast there is, the more shadow you have.

One of the masters of shadow working today is the American director David Fincher. Not only does he have great contrast in his shots, but there's contrast between shots of a scene, between shots of a sequence, and between sequences. Watch *The Girl with the Dragon Tattoo* (2011) and see how Fincher plays with the dark figures in the snow or goes from a shot that's mostly black into one that's completely the opposite. It's almost as if you were looking at a photographic negative of the previous shot.

Fincher has worked with some of the best cinematographers in the business, like Jeff Cronenweth, Darius Khondji, and the late Harris Savides. They're the ones responsible for crafting Fincher's vision into executable shots. A cinematographer's job is to paint with light, and the best ones can use light as methodically and subtly as a painter uses a brush.

The more shadows there are in a shot, the more aware the audience becomes that something dramatic is going on. In another excellent Fincher movie, *Gone Girl*, there's a great shot in which Ben Affleck is completely encased in shadow. He's just a perfect silhouette sitting on a chair, and you know instinctively that something dark is brewing inside him. Shadows litter the landscape of the film like hidden demons. It's beautiful filmmaking.

contrast

CASE STUDY: JAWS

Sometimes the best ideas come out of necessity. Spielberg had planned plenty of shark shots for the beginning of *Jaws*. Unfortunately, the mechanical shark constructed for this didn't work properly. Spielberg was already behind schedule when he came up with a solution: He wouldn't show the shark at all. Instead, he used Point of View (POV) shots of the shark looking up at the swimming bodies on the surface of the water. These shots, combined with the actors' reactions and John Williams's haunting score, make for some of the most terrifying moments in movie history. Instead of seeing this lumbering mechanical shark that didn't move like a real shark at all, we imagine what the monster would look like—and, of course, we picture the worst.

The agile camera

The camera should be agile and fluid, moving from place to place almost imperceptibly. If your edit and your camerawork are right, often the audience can't even tell when the cut happened.

The camera should be so agile that you anticipate what the audience will want to see even before they want it. A great example of this is a scene in *No Country for Old Men,* by the Coen brothers. It's the scene in which Anton Chigurh tracks down Llewelyn Moss to the Eagle Motel. Moss figures out that there's a transmitter in the bag of money he's got. This is the way the hitmen have been tailing him all along. Although he has discovered that, it's too late: Chigurh is already on him. Moss turns the lights off in his room and points his shotgun at the door. Chigurh is outside.

The Coen brothers do a fantastic job with the sequence of shots in this scene, which is experienced from Moss's point of view, as he's the one trying to avoid getting killed. A few times the camera gets to where Moss's going to be before he does, showing the audience exactly what they would want to see even before the subject gets there. The camera goes to the thin line of light below the door before Moss goes down to look through and see if there's anybody outside. Then the camera goes to the bag where the shotgun is, right before Moss goes to get it. The Coens' camera is fluid and fast. In anticipating our reactions, it heightens the emotional involvement of the audience. Just as you think, "Get the shotgun! He's outside!", you discover that the Coens are already there.

The sequence of shots is dynamic, mimicking the drama and tension of the scene. This is an intense moment, in which our protagonist almost gets murdered. There's a moment when he's running for his life and gets to the corner of a street. When he looks down the avenue, the Coens go to a POV shot of the empty street. Next they return to Moss at the corner, in pain because he's already been shot, and hoping to find some way of escape. Then back to the street where a lonely pickup truck lumbers down the avenue. Moss goes for it. The Coens cut to an overhead shot so we can see our protagonist begin to cross. Next, a moving shot of his boots crossing the street, then the window of the truck where he appears and tells the driver he's not going to hurt him as he gets in, bloody and carrying the shotgun. Then the reverse of the driver staring at him, looking scared, when all of a sudden a bullet cuts through the driver's neck. The man gets shot a few more times until Moss gets hold of the wheel and manages to drive away under a barrage of gunfire.

It's a masterfully crafted scene. At no point do the Coens remind you that you're watching a movie by adding odd shots or angles that are not necessary or by calling attention to themselves. They show you exactly what you need to see and they do so when you need to see it. Nothing more. No fancy rotating camera angles that would only serve to distract. Simple filmmaking tells the story—simple yet complex, because of its composition, lighting, and content. The shots are dynamic, beautiful, and practical, and they fit perfectly with the context, style, and narrative of the film.

The mind's eye

At its core, camerawork reveals what your head sees when it thinks about the scene. If I asked you to describe to me your favorite restaurant, you might start by telling me about where it is and how you get there, followed by what the atmosphere is inside and what the decor is like. Then you would probably tell me about the food and what you usually order when you're there. What you just did was give me a series of shots of how you see the place. If you ever were to shoot a scene at that very restaurant, you'd probably shoot it just like you described it.

Let your mind's eye tell you where it wants to go and you'll discover your own style of shooting. There's magic in what your imagination wants to see. Listen to it. After all, when you see a filmmaker's best work, what you're actually seeing is how they dream, a window onto their subconscious. That's what filmmakers do: bring dreams to life.

CASE STUDY: KUBRICK

One of the most talented filmmakers of all time, Stanley Kubrick loved using **one-point perspective**, which means that in the shot all the longitudinal lines converge at a central point, known as the **vanishing point**. The shots are done with near perfect symmetry. If you're looking down a long corridor, longitudinal lines are the lines where ceiling and floor meet walls. It would look something like the image opposite.

However, in order for this to be just right, you'll have to lower your head by about 1ft (30cm). Now you're seeing the world from the vantage point of a child. With one shot, Kubrick has taken you back to childhood. If that's not genius, I don't know what is.

LIFE ON THE SET
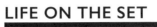

equipment

A friend once said to me, "A day on set beats a day in a cubicle, any day." If you decide on a career in filmmaking, you will spend a lot of time on set. Some people love it, while others hate it. Wonderful, creative things happen on set, but it can also be a place of discomfort, where you spend hours in a hot room, working with people you don't like, laboring on a project that you know from the get-go is not going anywhere. When that happens, it can really drain your creative energies and leave you wondering why you chose this path in the first place. But just remember that movies are like friends—every experience is different. Approach each one fresh and ready to do your job.

Starting out as a crew member

If you've decided to do this for a living, you'll start at the bottom. That means you'll be a production assistant, a grip, or perhaps a second or third AC (assistant camera) or AD (assistant director). You'll be carrying equipment, rolling cable, dressing the set, getting coffee, making runs to the store for supplies, covering windows with duvetyn (to block light), holding bounce boards (to reflect light), setting up the camera, pushing the dolly, and/or driving the van. It can be an exciting job and fulfilling. You'll meet a lot of people, some of them good and some not so good at what they do.

Learn what your duties are and stick to them. Learn how to roll cable. Find out how to set up a C-stand correctly. Learn the names of the different pieces of G&E (grip and electric) equipment. Be on time. Never complain. Always bring good energy to the set. And when you're not needed, disappear into the background like a ninja.

When you shadow or assist somebody, work out how that person works. Find out what they like. Learn their habits. Be ready with the equipment they'll need. If you're an assistant camera, pay attention to the director of photography. Your job is to serve him or her. You must have what they need, when they need it, and set it up properly. You may get to have some creative input but don't count on it. You're there to serve and facilitate, so do this to the best of your ability.

Pay attention. When the director and the DP (director of photography) rehearse a scene, watch and listen to what's going on. Most of what you need to know to do your job will be talked about. Listen to what the DP wants to do with the lights, and watch where the actors will be moving and where the camera will be. You'll get a sense of where the lights need to be placed, where the boom operator has to stand, what lens they'll use. There's nothing better than a crew member who pays attention. Creatives don't want to have to repeat the same instruction ten times. If the DP says they want a 2K through the window with CTB and they want it flagged from the actor's face with the solid, you will snap to get the stuff they need to make it happen right away. (And you will know that a 2K is a 2000kW light, CTB is a Color Temperature Blue color correction gel, and flagging with a solid is cutting the light completely.) But if you were looking at your phone when the conversation happened between director and DP, then you're just slowing everything down. Now the gaffer will have to explain the entire shot to you again.

So remember, if you're a crew member, you're there to serve the collective good of the project and to shadow someone. Do your job and only your job— and know what that is. Maintain a good attitude, pay attention, be selfless, and never complain.

Being on set can be challenging. It can be hot and crowded, or cold and lonesome. You may have to be on your feet all day, carry equipment for long distances, eat cold pizza, and drink warm soda. You may have to deal with crew members who don't know their jobs or you don't get along with, who don't like the same kind of movies you like, who think they know everything, or who have different political views. But all this will be easier to put up with if you fall in love with the grind.

Getting known

Making movies is hard enough, but once you get known as somebody who's a pleasure to have on set, you'll get hired again and again. If you're lucky, you'll become part of somebody's crew. Unit production managers have their crews of ADs and PAs. Directors of photography have their crews of ACs and gaffers and grips. Production designers have their own set designers, decorators, and set dressers. People like to work with the same folks over and over, so once you're in, you'll move up within these crews, and your experience and knowledge will grow.

Little by little, you'll start learning different setups and tricks. You'll learn how to solve creative problems. Each situation is different, so the more experience you have, the more desirable a crew member you'll become.

Being on set is the finishing school to your education as a filmmaker. Stella Adler (founder of New York's Stella Adler Studio of Acting) used to say that it took two years for an actor to learn the technique. Then they needed to go out and do 20 plays – and only then could they call themselves an actor. Being a crew member is much the same thing. You finish

film school, then you go out on set and work 20
productions; until you've done that, you don't really
know what you're doing. There is no substitute for
experience, no easy shortcut.

An experienced and dedicated crew member is hard
to come by. But once you are in that enviable position,
you'll find that the fun and satisfaction of the creative
process more than compensate for the hardship of
working on the set.

WHAT ABOUT THE PAY?

If you're working on independent films, don't expect
to make a lot of money. This is the type of thing you
do because you love it and because you want to learn.
To make a living from it, you'll have to work a lot and
go from set to set. Develop a good reputation and it'll
happen. Once you start to work on larger sets, then
the pay will get better. If you're a technician working
on a Hollywood set or the set of a major show, then
you'll be making a good living.

A word to the wise

If you discover along the way that there are positions
you really like and that you're good at, listen to your
inner voice. Most people who go to film school set
out to become a director, but some people discover
halfway through that they're not really suited to
directing. They realize that what they really like is
set design, or sound, or cinematography, or dolly
gripping. Whatever it is, listen to your inner voice.
This isn't always easy—everybody thinks that being
a director is the ultimate, and they don't want to
give up on that dream. But a set only works because
everybody does their job. Every position has its own
importance. If you find out that you're really good
at, say, production design, don't be afraid to change
direction. We don't need any more directors that
"kind of" want to direct. What we need is production
designers who love what they do.

discover

It's difficult to accept that your childhood dream was just that, a childhood dream, but life changes. You learn new things about yourself and about the job. Don't discard those things because you had set out to do something different. What you had set out to do might have been right at that time, but now you're a different person. You know more, and you're more mature. Your inner voice will tell you where your talent lies, so follow that voice.

When serendipity happens

One of my first-ever students got assigned the role of sound during a production workshop. He didn't really want to do it but it was the position that needed filling, so he did it. In the process he discovered he was good at it and he liked it. He had started out wanting to be a director, but there were a lot of things about directing that weren't sitting right with him, like having to keep coming up with ideas for movies one after the other, which stressed him out. Yet he enjoyed concentrating on his equipment and doing his job right, and he found that working in sound took a huge weight from his shoulders. It allowed him to have fun and to become really good at something.

In fact, he became excellent at it and is now one of the best soundmen I know, traveling all over the world doing it. He's a pleasure to work with. You set up a scene and he's listening. He knows where he needs to be to capture the sound but be out of the way. An awesome technician, he's developed a reputation for precision, reliability, and having a good attitude. I don't think he's stopped working since he graduated. Imagine if he had stuck to directing— he probably wouldn't be in the business by now.

A set can be a wonderful place of learning, not only about the craft of filmmaking, but also about yourself. Filmmaking is one of the few endeavors that taxes you at all levels, and the set is where this happens. Keep your ears and eyes open.

WHATEVER IT TAKES

I knew I wanted to be a director from the start, but I worked for ABC News for ten years first. The things I learned prepared me for the movie set better than any other job could have. I was a production assistant with ABC when 9/11 happened. One evening about a week later, we were broadcasting when two men in what looked like astronaut suits opened the door of my control-room booth and announced, "There's anthrax in the building. Please don't move, as we have to determine where it is." The operator in the booth next to mine fainted but another was brought in to replace her, and we stayed on the air. I had a job to do and I was going to do it, no matter what.

"But I really want to be a director!"

Fantastic, then that's what you should do. But don't expect to move up from being a PA straight to directing. Don't assume that someday somebody's going to say to you, "Okay, now's your turn. You'll direct the next one." Nobody's ever going to hand it to you on a plate—you'll have to do it yourself.

So if you want to be a director, go and direct. Get your own crew together and make your own projects. You'll meet a lot of the people who will help you while you're on set doing other things. Most will have their own projects they're working on, and if they enjoy working with you, they may hire you to work on their film. If you like them, then you'll probably hire them to work on yours. And so it goes.

Set life can be extremely fulfilling. And even though it's not as glamorous as most people think it is, I agree with the friend I mentioned earlier: It does beat a day in a cubicle, any day.

director

PRODUCTION DESIGN

Part of what we do in filmmaking is to access the parts of the brain that control emotions, without having to go through the parts that control judgment. It actually does work. Imagine that a monster's face appears on the screen and the viewers jump. They react even though they don't want to. For us filmmakers, this is gold. Their reaction is pure, direct, and powerful. We want the audience to come on the story's emotional rollercoaster, but their critical faculties sometimes get in the way of that. Therefore filmmakers want to bypass the judgmental parts of the brain, which would protest that this is just a movie, these are just actors, and none of this is really happening. The bypass process is known as suspension of disbelief, and movies are the perfect medium for it.

Image systems

The masters of filmmaking, like Kubrick, Bergman, Kurosawa, Fellini, and others, understood well how suspension of disbelief could work in films. The filmmaker Tony Gilroy, an amazing artist, is known for his work adapting and directing the Jason Bourne movies, but in 2007 he wrote and directed a movie called *Michael Clayton*, which is a masterpiece. The acting is brilliant, the cinematography spot on, and the writing superb. But one of the elements that set *Michael Clayton* apart from other movies is its image system.

emotions

An **image system** is an image that's repeated throughout the film and has a significance. It can be a color, a theme, a play of shadows, a shape, an actual picture, an object, the weather, an element, a sound, a landscape. This image must blend into the background of the action of the film, so that it's just part of what you shot. And here's the kicker: The audience must not notice it is there. And, yes, I can hear you ask how they know to react. The answer is that they don't, but it doesn't matter—the important thing is that they're looking at it. They may not know they're being exposed to it but, just like a subliminal message, it makes its way into the brain.

Spoiler alert: If you haven't seen *Michael Clayton*, please stop reading right now and go watch it, to see if you can figure out what the image system is. Once I tell

you, it will lose its power, because your conscious brain can then analyze it, dissect it, and dismiss it. But while you're unaware of it, it can affect you without any filter.

So…the image system in *Michael Clayton* is the color red. My theory is that it is the color of truth, and, as the film's tagline clearly states, the truth can be adjusted. In this movie, every time a character is telling the truth, the color red appears; it is all over the film. And when the "bad guys" are on the screen, we don't see the color at all. It's a masterful piece of directing.

Another of my favorite image systems is in *The Truman Show*. This one is an image system of mirrors and reflections. I once counted 37 reflections in one scene alone. *The Truman Show* is about a character who's part of a television program but doesn't know it—

he is totally unaware of who he really is. Do you
think reflections are a powerful metaphor for this
character's predicament?

Editing

It wasn't until Edwin S. Porter, an employee of
Thomas Edison (another one of the inventors of the
movie camera), discovered editing that films became
a thing to watch. Porter figured out that by cutting
pieces of different reels of film together, you could
tell stories. He and some of the other visionaries of
film invented, mostly by trial and error, what we now
call film language.

In one of his first films, Porter cut together footage
of a house on fire and then footage of firemen getting
into their truck. Then he went back to the house on
fire and a woman on the second floor screaming to
be saved. Then back to the firemen, already on their
truck and racing down the street. Then back to
the fire and so on. Where's the fire truck going?
To the fire, of course. How do you know that? You
assume. And that's one of the most incredible things
about film—your brain does half the work all on
its own. I juxtapose two things and you make the
connection. When Porter made those cuts between
fire and firemen, he didn't know that audiences were
going to make that assumption. At least he wasn't
sure. In his own head, it worked, so he took a chance.

The 20th-century Russian filmmaker Lev Kuleshov
did a number of experiments with film and editing,
and one in particular has become quite famous. He
photographed a Russian matinee idol in a close-up.
Next, he cut together the close-up of this man with
other footage, of a bowl of steaming soup, a girl
playing with a teddy bear, and a woman crying over
a coffin. He then showed this footage to audiences.

juxtapose

Close-up to bowl of soup. Close-up to little girl. Close-up to coffin. Audiences raved about the acting. They said they could feel the hunger when the man was looking at the bowl of soup, the tenderness when he was looking at the little girl, and the pain he felt at the woman crying over her husband's coffin.

In fact, the actor was never told what he was supposed to be looking at and, what's more, it was exactly the same shot of the actor all three times. This is now known as the **Kuleshov effect** and it means that one image has a meaning and another has a second meaning, but when they are cut together, a third meaning arises—a meaning that emerges from the minds of the audience.

We are constantly seeking an explanation for what we see, even if we're not aware that we're seeing it. That is how our brains work. The power of film can be overwhelming, and the masters learned how to use it and how to manipulate our emotional state with the images on the screen.

CASE STUDY: MONOLITH AND METAPHOR

In *2001: A Space Odyssey*, Stanley Kubrick introduced a monolith in the scene at the beginning of the movie when cavemen are fighting over a water hole. Following the appearance of the black monolith, a caveman employs a bone as a weapon, properly thinking for the first time. The monolith can be seen as a metaphor for reason.

In Kubrick's later film *Full Metal Jacket*, set during the Vietnam War, a character named Cowboy is dying. Cowboy represents reason. During his death scene, a ruined building on fire in the background resembles the monolith from *2001*. Kubrick claimed that any resemblance was "an extraordinary coincidence", but if you are familiar with how methodical he was, you'll know this was *not* a coincidence. Kubrick is showing us the death of reason.

Wish fulfillment

If images are the drugs of the subconscious, directors are the pushers. Filmmakers must access the portion of the brain that controls emotion. You must make the audience feel. That's why they go to the cinema, to experience emotions they don't have in real life, and do so in a safe environment.

I often ask my students why they think *Titanic* was one of the most successful films of all time. The answer is simple: We all wish we had a love that would give their life for us. We buy our ticket and Leonardo DiCaprio does it for us—and looks better doing it as well. What's more, if we watch the movie over and over, he does it again and again. It's marvelous.

As a director, it is your job to master the tools of your trade. You're providing the audience with something they can't get any other way. Everything you put on the screen will affect them in one way or another. If you do it well, they'll love you for it. It's okay if every once in a while you have to trick them to do it.

Production design doesn't happen by coincidence: It happens by choice, so make sure you choose wisely. Remember, the devil's in the details—especially those of which the audience are not necessarily aware.

ACTORS

inspiration

One of the toughest realities to accept in film is that you can't make a movie alone. This is particularly hard for people who are independent and enjoy living in the world of the imagination. Of course, these are the people who gravitate toward filmmaking.

Direction and inspiration

To make movies you need a number of other artists to help you create the illusions of film. A useful talent for a director to possess is to be able to get others to do their best work for them. Not an easy task for anyone, let alone a person who has retreated into the world of their imagination. And that's the real trick. The director must be able to wear all these different hats. When you're conceptualizing the film, you have to imagine what the film will look like before you shoot a single frame. Then, at some point, you must reach out to others and convince them to be part of your madness for a little while. You must be an introvert and an extrovert simultaneously.

The other artists most directly responsible for carrying the illusion of the film on their shoulders are the actors. Their faces are enlarged to a colossal size on that screen. They're the ones who bring forth the emotional life of the movie and who have to pretend to be somebody else for people to buy into your story. Working with actors is one of the most important and yet neglected parts of directing.

In film school, you spend most of the time working on the technical aspects of the art form. There's a lot to learn and it can get overwhelming. It's been my experience that those who are studying directing tend to concentrate on this technical side and lose sight of the collaboration that has to take place. Not only are actors some of the most important artists you'll work with in the process of making your film but they're also the most powerful people in Hollywood.

Only two things are used to advertise a movie: the faces of the actors and the budget. The actors and whatever special effects the movie is trying to sell are all you see in the posters and in the trailers. Actors and spectacle.

If you become known as a director who's really good at working with actors, you've got it made. If a movie star decides they love working with you, then you've just won the lottery. You'll have a much easier time getting your projects made.

CASE STUDY: SCORSESE

Martin Scorsese is known for creating the best atmosphere on set for actors to do their job. Actors are keen to work with him because they know they're going to do some great work. That's why he's had long collaborations with some of the best actors in Hollywood. James Woods is said to have left a telephone message for Scorsese saying, "Any part, any time, any price, anywhere." That's a director who understands how important actors are to the process and that it's his job to make it easier for them to do theirs.

Showing emotion

In order to understand how a director works with actors, we must first understand what actors are trying to achieve. I tell all my students that they are in a service industry. People go to the movies to get what they're not getting in real life. For two hours, the lights go down and you become Indiana Jones, or the Dark Knight, or Hannibal Lecter. But in order for that magic to happen, the emotions the actors are feeling on the screen must be real. So how do we know if they are?

It's because we can feel them, rather like the phenomenon known as sympathetic resonance in music—if you have two pianos tuned the same way in a room and you hit a key on one, the same note resonates in the other. Similarly, when one human is vibrating with an emotion, the other human vibrates, too. We've all felt it at the theater, a concert, or a movie.

It's a wonderful mechanism, which makes this business of ours work. And just as it becomes your job to make it easier for the audience to have these emotions, it's also your responsibility to make it easier for the actors to have them. That's no picnic— think about what you're asking them to do. They have to have an emotion on demand, encumbered by all the pressures of filmmaking. And we're not talking about simple emotions, but the stuff of drama.

Stanislavski

If you've studied acting, you'll be familiar with the name Konstantin Stanislavski, the famous Russian acting teacher of the 1920s and 1930s. Most modern acting techniques derive from his. Stanislavski noticed that some actors were actually feeling the emotions of the play as they were acting. Before Stanislavski, the accepted mode of acting was what we call today presentational acting, in which an actor would "present" to you the emotion. In other words, they would pretend to have the emotion, and that would be enough indication for the audience. This was an accepted mode of acting at the time.

But what Stanislavski noticed is that some actors were actually *having* the emotions. The moments were real and therefore much more powerful. So he started interviewing these actors and asking them how they were achieving this.

Stanislavski wrote a number of books, but his seminal work was *An Actor's Work,* published in the US (in an abridged version) as *An Actor Prepares.* In it he presents an imaginary director going through a rehearsal process with a group of actors who ask him questions, and the director then gives them exercises to achieve the truthful moments of the play. This is an important book for both actors and directors to read.

Stanislavski went on to become one of the founders of the Moscow Art Theatre, and at some point he brought his actors to New York to perform some Chekhov plays. *The Three Sisters*, in particular, caused an uproar—New York actors had never seen performances like these.

Method acting

Lee Strasberg and Stella Adler, two members of a small New York collective of actors called the Group Theatre, decided to study Stanislavski's technique. They then taught it to the other members of the group, though each interpreted Stanislavski's teachings in their own way. Later, Sanford Meisner also became part of the group and started interpreting Stanislavski's teachings in his own way. Strasberg, Adler, and Meisner represent the three main branches (psychological, sociological,

and behavioral respectively) of what we call today
method acting, or **the Method**.

All three were concerned with bringing forth the
truth of the play and creating real emotions on stage
or on camera. To see masters of the three techniques
in the same movie, watch *The Godfather*. Al Pacino
studied with Strasberg (and Strasberg actually appears
in *The Godfather II*), Marlon Brando studied with
Adler, and Robert Duvall studied with Meisner. It's a
lot of fun to watch, not only because it's a marvelous
movie, but in terms of technique it's a treasure-trove.

Using action to create subtext

As I've said before, the camera loves subtext—when
an actor is saying one thing but has something else
happening underneath. Part of your job as a director
is to help actors create this subtext. So how do
directors encourage actors to achieve what they're
trying to do? One tool I recommend is **action**, which
is what an actor plays under the lines. It is often
expressed in verb form: to humiliate, to mock, to
teach, to seduce, to connive, to soften, all of which
are acting actions. An actor will pick one that they
believe is appropriate for a moment and they will play
it underneath the words they're saying.

Let's say the scene calls for a character to enter the
kitchen, where another character is having breakfast
at the counter. Then this first character goes to the
fridge, opens the door, looks inside, and has the line,
"Where's the milk?"

That's a fairly simple moment. However, we don't
know what's happening between these two people.
They could be brother and sister, lovers, strangers
who met just the night before, or perhaps employee
and boss. There are all kinds of possibilities.

Now let's create some subtext and add an action. Character A comes into the kitchen, where character B is having breakfast. Character A goes to the fridge, looks inside, and says: "Where's the milk?" Character A does the scene while playing the action *to seduce*.

While they are playing the action, everything they do is governed by it—how they enter, cross to the fridge, look at character B, open the fridge, say their line. The action colors what they do and say with subtext.

The words don't really matter that much. What matters is what the actors play underneath. Now go ahead and say that line, "Where's the milk?"

Say it using the action *to seduce*. Say it using the action *to humiliate*, or *to inspire*, or *to guilt-trip*. See how different the inflection is, and how your intention varies.

It may seem small to you but the camera picks up on everything. When that actor enters the room playing the action *to seduce*, opens the fridge, and says, "Where's the milk?", believe me, if they are a good actor we would know exactly what's going on. That's what the audience remembers anyway— they'll forget what the actors said almost as soon as they say it, but they'll remember what was going on for a long time after.

truthful

IT'S ALL IN THE EYES

I play a little game with my students, in which I remind
them of the scene in *Titanic* where Jack draws Rose
naked in her cabin, then I ask them what was said.
No one remembers that Jack and Rose talk about
her being a paying customer and Monet painting
landscapes. But who cares? What matters is what's
going on underneath. They're falling in love. This is
what the camera loves and this is what we remember.
It's all in the eyes—the camera cuts through and lets
us see what's inside.

Now let's go back to our little scene with the milk.
Character A walks in, playing the action *to seduce*, and
says, "Where's the milk?" Let's give Character B a line
as well. They say, "I don't know and I don't care." Let's
also give Character B an action: the action *to humiliate*.
So Character A walks in playing the action to seduce and
says, "Where's the milk?" Character B plays the action
to humiliate and says, "I don't know and I don't care."

There's a moment between them, and then they fall into each other's arms and devour each other on the kitchen counter.

Can you picture it? Can you see how the actions make the scene a lot more dynamic? This is what the camera loves, so you must infuse your scenes with this magic. It's what keeps us coming back to the movies.

Directing an actor is all about creating subtext and behavior. The one cardinal sin of directing actors is to specify a result—for example, to say to the actor that they should act angry or sad or happy.

It's counterintuitive because it seems that the easiest way to arrive at what we want is to tell the actor how they're feeling, but the problem with this is that it defeats the entire purpose of what we're doing. If we want to create true emotion and spontaneous behavior, then we can't give the actor a result. If I say to the actor, "You're happy in this scene," it will mean that the actor will try to give you the image they have in their head of what happy looks like—but the best they can do is give you an imitation of what happiness looks like. For some actors the imitation of happiness looks pretty good, but it'll never be truthful and spontaneous.

In order to arrive at the happiness spontaneously, you have to give the actors the ingredients. The actor cooks the ingredients and gives you back soup. It's the long way around, but it's the only way to get to the type of performance that will resonate with the audience and surprise them.

Another reason we don't give an actor a result is that ultimately it's a lie. Human beings rarely feel just one emotion at a time or what we would deem the appropriate emotion. How many times have you been in a situation where you're supposed to feel one way but that's the last thing coursing through your body?

At a funeral? In bed with your lover?

An emotion is so much more complex than just the word we assign to it. If you tell the actor how they feel, then you're oversimplifying human experience and reducing an emotion to a mere word.

What you need to do is give the actor the circumstances and let them immerse themselves in the situation and act honestly. If emotion arises, great, but if it doesn't, so be it.

Of course, here comes the disclaimer...there are some exceptional actors to whom you can give a result and they will still immerse themselves in the circumstances and give you a good, truthful performance. But that's rare and you're playing with fire. My advice is not to do it unless you've worked with the actor before and you know they can take the instruction and fly with it. For every other actor, give them an action. This is the subtext of what they're doing and it governs their behavior during the scene.

A scene may have one, two, three, twenty actions. It can have an action for each beat—a **scene beat** is, in fact, a moment of action and reaction.

WHATEVER TURNS YOU ON
The members of the Atlantic Theater Company, an Off-Broadway nonprofit theater in Manhattan, have written a little book called *A Practical Handbook for the Actor*. It provides lots of great advice for actors, including how to pick a good acting action. One of their principal guidelines is that a good action must "turn you on." If this makes you think of making out in the back of a car, that's exactly the appropriate reaction. Whatever choice you make for an acting action must activate the actor. How can they hope to make the audience feel something, if the actor doesn't feel anything?

An actor's means of expression—their body, senses, mind, emotion, imagination, and empathy—is sometimes called the actor's **instrument**. Their instrument must be switched on. Stella Adler used to say that "an actor is always shopping." Shopping for what? For things that activate their instrument. When an actor comes across one of these, they file it in their little bag of tricks to be used at a later date.

Like a musician, the actor needs their instrument to be alive if they hope to awaken the audience. One of the hardest things you'll do as a director is tell an actor that whatever choice they're making is not really doing anything for them, or at least not enough. But you must do that if you want to help them give you a good performance.

And how would you know if the choice the actor is making is turning them on? Because you would feel it, just like the audience would. I suggest that in your own work you follow the advice of the founders of the Atlantic Theater Company. If your choices as a director don't turn you on, then how can you hope to turn others on to your work?

Obstacle and circumstance

So you give an actor an action, which should give them
the subtext. But the action is only the beginning of the
process. It's just one of the ingredients—there are
two other useful tools.

Here's a bit of direction. You say to Actor A that
Actor B in this scene has a bag full of money that
Actor A wants. Their objective in the scene is to
get the bag of money. So you tell Actor A that he
will play the action to seduce Actor B to get that bag.

The second tool for creating subtext is the **obstacle**.
You say to Actor A that you want this bag and you
will play the action to seduce—however, Actor B is
disgusting to you and makes you feel sick. That should
make for some interesting behavior.

The obstacle works in opposition to the action.
And it's there just to create behavior, to produce a
dramatic situation.

A third tool for creating subtext is the **circumstance**,
or what many acting techniques call the magic "as if."
You say to Actor A that they need that bag of money.
They will play the action to seduce to get it from
Actor B. However, Actor B is disgusting to them and
makes them feel sick. Here's another obstacle: You
say to Actor A that they're drunk. That makes it even
more difficult. Then you add the cherry on top: You
tell them that the cops are going to burst through
the door any second now and arrest them, and they
must get that money before this happens. Their lives
depend on it. Go! That's how you direct an actor.

CASE STUDY: THE MAGIC OF BRANDO

When I was studying acting, Marlon Brando was considered by many to be the pinnacle of the art form, the greatest American actor who ever lived, the embodiment of method acting (see pages 93–4). What distinguished Brando from other actors was his ability to let himself be. When you watch movies like *On the Waterfront*, *The Wild One,* and *Apocalypse Now*, what you see is a performer totally comfortable with letting the camera in. He doesn't have to do anything. He doesn't have to act, or have some kind of emotional moment, or pretend. He can just be relaxed in front of the camera. I find that fact extremely telling about the level Brando was able to achieve.

His teacher, Stella Adler, has been quoted as saying, "Acting is doing." To her, an actor was always doing something and that was reflected in her technique and the use of actions. Actors always need to be aware of the action they're playing, yet Brando seemed able to be in front of the camera without having to do anything. But that's deceptive. He had gotten so good at being relaxed in front of the camera that he *was* doing something, it just wasn't apparent. He was being.

Brando became famous on Broadway when he played Stanley Kowalski in Tennessee Williams's *A Streetcar Named Desire*. Legend has it that when Brando made his entrances, the audience thought he was a stagehand who had just wandered on. That's how relaxed he was.

At his best he was a riveting performer. There's a scene in *On the Waterfront* when two policemen come to confront him on the docks and one of them is standing behind him while the other one's in front. Brando looks like a caged animal. He doesn't know whether to turn to one cop or the other, whether to answer their questions or smack them in the mouth and run. He doesn't know and so we don't know either. We're glued to that screen to see what's going to happen next. It's the ultimate in truthful and spontaneous behavior.

Adler used to get her classes to do an exercise in which she would place a number of props (a cup of coffee, a glove, some money) in front of an actor and have them play with the props while they were doing the scene. Called "What Things Do," the exercise was designed to have the actor connect with the truth of the moment through an inanimate object. The point was that you may not be able to give me the truth while acting, but at least you won't be lying with regard to this prop. It means something to you, it has an association. A chair is for sitting. Its use is part of its meaning.

In *On the Waterfront*, Brando has a scene with the love interest, a character named Edie, played by Eva Marie Saint, in her feature film debut. They're sitting on a swing-set in a park, and the actress drops one of her gloves by mistake. Brando immediately takes it in his hands and starts to play with it, just as he did in the exercise in the acting class. He puts it on. He plays with the fingers. Elia Kazan, the director, who had been a member of the Group Theatre as well, and who knew Adler's technique, was smart enough to leave the moment in. It's Brando at his best—a master craftsman at work.

Understanding the subtext

You already know that movie scenes are often written away from what's really going on because we want to give the actors subtext to play. So a scene that's about two characters falling in love will rarely have the words "I love you" in it. It'll be something like the scene in *Titanic* where Jack draws Rose (see page 96).

In the scene in *Pulp Fiction* where Mia thanks Vincent for saving her life, she never actually says the words "thank you." This is the way good movie scenes are written: The best ones always have subtext built in. What movie scenes do is mimic reality—most of the things we do in real life have subtext. In addition, what we say can have an infinite number of meanings, and be different from the meaning someone else attaches to the same words.

When directing actors, make sure you know what the subtext of the scene is. If there's a hidden agenda under the lines, you need to know it. It'll give the actors' performances a purpose and your relationship with the actors a strong foundation. Make them feel that you and they know something that nobody else does—it'll supercharge their performance and make them more confident and relaxed on camera.

Shooting emotional scenes

Don't forget that part of your job as a director is to make it easier for the actor to give you their best performance. Give them the time they need.

Make the AD (assistant director) aware of the shot in which you're going to record the emotional moment—a good AD will know this anyway. Give the actor advance notice of when this shot will be done, as well as some extra time and a private space for them to prepare.

Light the scene with a stand-in and let the actors work on themselves. Make sure you're lit and ready to go. That doesn't mean almost ready! Remember that film crews and DPs (directors of photography) are notorious for being almost ready. The last thing you want is the actors standing around waiting for lights to be adjusted when they're holding on to this big emotional moment. You're just making it harder on them to give you what you want. Only when you're certain you're ready do you bring the actor in to do their take.

Make sure the crew is quiet and concentrating, with no joking around. Crews get looser as production goes on. It's natural, as everyone is under pressure and in an enclosed space, so they need to let off some steam. It tends to happen late in the production and late in the day, when everyone is tired and when maintaining concentration is difficult. The actors will be open and letting emotions fly, and the crew will be affected by that and whatever else is happening around them, including antics on the set.

And, of course, when focus is loose is usually when this type of shot takes place. It's late in the day and here it comes, the big monologue where the actor is expected to have their emotional outburst. But a shot with some strong emotional content is when the crew will need their concentration the most. Watch out for that moment, and stay on top of it.

Seeing what happens

Every once in a while you'll come across an actor who's fighting you on something. You want them to go in one direction but they want to go in a completely different one. My advice is to let the actor go the way they want and see what happens. They may come up with something that you hadn't thought of. Here's the fun thing about that: You can take credit for it later on!

Remember that you're working with actors, not puppets. They'll have their own interpretation of what's going on, and it's your job to reach an accord. At any rate, an actor's interpretation may surprise you, so

production

remain open—art is about transformation. If you don't open up to the process, your art will never grow; you'll have said all you have to say with one film and that'll be the end of your useful contribution to the world.

Useful tricks

All directors have various tricks up their sleeve for getting the best out of their actors. Here are a few of mine.

Give them the credit

Let's say that the actor's performance is not going as planned and you really want them to go in a different direction. Perhaps they can't reach the emotional point

you wanted. Perhaps they don't really understand the
role, or the moment, or the script. Maybe they're
not talented enough to do it—that's a tough one,
especially if you both realize this as rehearsal goes on.
Or sometimes you're working with a powerful movie
star, and you can't really tell them what to do.

Here's a little trick to use in those situations. (Some
people will hate me for this, but it's harmless and I've
used it in many ways.) Make them think the change is
coming from them.

When they're done with the take you say, "That
was wonderful. When you told her how you felt
this time, it was like you were talking to your own
daughter. It was masterful. Let's do another and
explore that. Go more in that direction, like you're
talking to your daughter, just to have options."
Then you go again.

Of course, nothing they did really prompted that. It's
just what you want. You're just giving them credit for
it. Who cares who gets the credit for anything? Keep
your eye on the doughnut and not the hole. Get your
movie made the way you want it.

Make love to the camera
Sometimes you'll come across actors who get self-
conscious when the camera starts rolling. They're fine
during the audition and in rehearsal, but as soon as
the camera rolls they start "acting."

talented

A good way to deal with this is to explain to them that they should think of working with the camera as being like flirting with someone. Flirting involves all kinds of actions and allowances, but ultimately opens doors; you're allowing the person access to the private you, in an unspoken exchange of allowances.

Let's say you're in a crowded bar. A person you like walks in. Although you're standing all the way across the room, you immediately open up a channel of communication with that person. You're not doing anything but just letting them in. That's the way actors can work with the camera.

Working with the camera is much more about letting things happen than doing something with it. I often say to my students that you have to make love to the camera—it's an intimate relationship.

Move their focus away from themselves
Sometimes you'll encounter an actor who's listening to their own voice or watching themselves move. You'll notice it. The tone of their voice changes from the one they use to talk to you, which is a dead giveaway.

It's a false moment, and you don't want any false moments in your film. You should have a little lie detector in your brain that sounds the alarm when an actor hits a false moment.

The first thing to do is to tell them to think of nothing else but the other actor, to observe what the other actor is doing in minute detail. Tell them you're going to ask them questions about it at the end. That take will probably not have exactly what you want, but at least you will have gotten the actor out of their own head, allowing the performance of the other actor to shape what they're doing.

Have a banal chat

Here's another trick if an actor keeps changing their tone of voice: Have a totally banal conversation with them. Get really close and ask them what they had for breakfast. Did they like it? What about their commute? What car do they drive? It should be an intimate, quiet little conversation between the two of you. Then, in the middle of that, without warning, have them jump into the scene. Their voice should maintain the same quality as when they were talking to you. If they go back to their "acting" voice, then you do it again until they can tell the difference.

Hire a pro

I say this over and over to my students: Hire a trained actor. If you hire an actor to play a cop, you'll get a decent-enough cop. If you hire a cop to play a cop, you'll get the worst actor in the world.

Always audition, and always give direction when you audition. Casting is half the battle. You want to know that your actor can tackle the demands of the role, and you're not going to know that if you hire a friend or somebody who was just recommended or, worse still, convenient. Audition!

casting

Preparing to audition

Some directors, especially student directors, hate casting, but it's an essential part of the process. So, how do you prepare to audition the actors?

Make sure you have a camera and, if possible, a monitor there. The monitor should be facing you and the actor should not be able to see themselves on camera. If you don't have a monitor, you'll need to record the audition. You'll need somebody operating the camera and, ideally, also somebody to read with the actor. The person reading shouldn't be you— you need to pay attention.

Send the **sides** (the pocket-size scripts for the scenes you'll be doing) to the actors in advance, at least the night before, so they can prepare for the audition. A good actor should be able to make decisions on the fly, if you were to give them the sides only on the day, but it's better if you allow them some time.

Remember that you're auditioning an actor for a role, but at the same time they're auditioning you. If an actor is given an audition time of 1:30, and if they get there to find that you have a group of actors waiting and you don't get to see them till 2:30 or 3:00, that tells the actor something. It suggests that if you can't run an audition on time, then you're likely to be even worse on set, and their time will be better served on another project.

Keep your schedule tight. Give the actors 10- or 15-minute slots. That will tell the actor you're an organized person and likely to be an efficient director.

Let's say that the actor has a 1:30 appointment. They show up at 1:15 and they wait. You should have a sign-up sheet where actors can write their appointment time and the time they arrive. If the actor has a time of 1:30 and they show up at 2:00, that tells *you*

something. If the actor really fits the role and they do a great audition, you might give them a second chance, but be very wary of people who can't be on time.

Warming up
The actor comes into the audition room. Remember that this is a nerve-racking situation for them. Some actors are great at auditioning, but others aren't. That doesn't mean they're bad actors, it just means they haven't mastered that aspect of it yet. Some actors may never master it—it's a hard thing to do.

Make them as comfortable as possible. Chat a little bit, read their resumé, ask about something they've done in the past. How was it working with this director or in that movie? Have they been doing this long? All you need is a couple of minutes. As much as possible, give them the opportunity to relax.

Then ask whether they have any questions for you. That's the cue to the actor that you're about to begin. If the actor does have questions, answer as truthfully as you can. They will probably be questions about the situation or the background of the character.

Reading the scene
Now let the actor read the scene, in the way they want to, with their own choices and interpretation.

You should be looking at the monitor and not the actor. You need to see what they look like on camera and how their performance translates to the screen. The camera loves some actors and it doesn't really care for others—it's a weird thing. In any case, what you need is for their performance to read on camera.

After they read, compliment them. Make them relax some more. You don't need to make a big deal out of it—just say, "Good job." Then you do it again, except this time you give them some kind of direction. Even if the actor nailed it the first time, you always give them direction.

choices

And what direction do you give? Simple: Give them an action to play or an obstacle, or change the circumstances. This is language the actor should understand and adjustments they should be able to make immediately.

You always give direction for two main reasons. First, you want to know if the actor has been trained and, second, you want to make sure they can take direction. Both pieces of information are crucial.

If you're auditioning a lead, pick two good scenes from the script. One should have a low emotional content and the other one high, the highest in the script. You do the one that's low to see if the actor can carry a normal scene without overacting. You want them to be able to just be in front of the camera and appear normal. A lot of actors who have trained extensively in the theater have trouble making that adjustment. They give you too much and it's apparent immediately in front of the camera. The other scene you do so you know if they can hit the big emotional note in the script. Perhaps they don't hit it perfectly, but they should be able to get close—close enough that you know that with some direction they'll hit it.

Let's face it, movies tend to be about one scene, the climax of act three. If the actor can't pull it off, then there's no point.

scenes

After the event

When they're done, don't tell them if they got the part—even if they rocked and you know you want to hire them. Ask them if they're available for the schedule, thank them, and send them on their way.

No matter how good somebody is, there might be somebody better auditioning right after them. Make your decision only after you've seen everybody.

Be prepared to do several auditions to find the person you want. This is a process, so wait to find the right person. Don't panic if nobody in your first audition is right for the parts. It took George Lucas almost a year to cast *Star Wars*. He did it with his friend Brian De Palma, who was casting for *Carrie*. Together they saw hundreds of actors before making choices.

When you've seen everyone and have found the right person, give them a call that night. You don't need to call all the other actors who auditioned, but you can send them an email thanking them if you want to. That would be nice but not necessary. They're actors—they don't need you to baby them.

The callback

Sometimes you can't tell from just one audition whether a person's right. For some roles, you need to see what the chemistry is with an actor playing another key role. For that you do a callback.

Tell the actors you'll need around a half hour for the callback. Call several actors together for the same time, and have them come in and read together. You may have three or four people for the same couple of roles, then you mix and match. Have them come in and read the scene, then step outside and come in again to read the same scene with a different partner.

All of these actors could possibly play the part, so now you want to see how they play off each other. Some actors have chemistry together, especially if they're playing love interests. The camera loves nothing better than built-in subtext, so if the actors like each other, that's a plus.

process

Rehearsals

I recommend at least three rehearsals whenever possible. This can be difficult to achieve in the film industry, especially as you progress and your budgets and the quality of your performers rise. Actors, especially movie stars, have busy schedules. To get them for rehearsal before a shoot can sometimes be impossible.

■ At the **first rehearsal** you'll read through the script a few times and answer questions about the situation and the background of the characters. Presumably your characters had lives before the events of the film took place, and actors will be curious about this past. Answer as best you can, even if you have not thought about it much. If you don't have an answer, let the actor come up with their own. They know their instrument and what works for them. By the end of this process the actors will know their characters better than you— even though you wrote them. That's all they'll do, think about their character, so it makes sense. This is also a good rehearsal for your costume designer to get measurements.

■ At the **second rehearsal** you get the actors on their feet, going through the scenes. At first let them move around as they want—it may give you ideas about how to block the scene. **Blocking the scene** is setting the movements of the actors and the camera. If you can, have your DP there for this rehearsal. By the end of it, the blocking should be pretty much set and the actors should know how they'll move in each scene. It also helps if they know what kinds of shots you'll be doing when they play each moment.

■ The **third rehearsal** should be a dress rehearsal. That means the actors do their scenes in full costume and ideally on location (which is not always possible). Don't wait until the day of the shoot to try out costumes. If something doesn't fit or is uncomfortable, you need to know, especially if an actor is wearing a wig or mask or something that may impede their performance. Try it out first so that there are no surprises on the shoot.

The purpose of these rehearsals is to work out each moment before principal photography. While you're on set, you'll have no time to be figuring out with the actors what a moment is about. All of that should be done beforehand. During the shoot you'll have plenty of technical problems and concerns you'll have to address.

Know what each moment is about. It's fine if the actors need refreshing on set. You can always refer them back to something they did during rehearsal.

In this way you can concentrate on getting beautiful images during the shoot. The better prepared you are, the more smoothly things will go and the better you'll be able to handle the curveballs that come your way—in production nothing ever goes as planned. The more confident you are of your material, the more adept you'll be at handling those things that go wrong while you're shooting. You'll handle them like a pro, which is what the crew and the cast will be looking for: a leader who knows how to hold their own under pressure.

rehearsal

POSTPRODUCTION

Movies are made three times. That's why, whatever the subject you choose for your film, you'd better be completely sure it's something you like, as you're going to have to live with it for a long time. You'll have to learn to make it, break it, and then make it again. This process of having to reinvent your material over and over is a good thing. It allows for the honing of the idea to its essence, losing all those insubstantial things that had no business being in the story to begin with.

Do yourself a favor and take good notes during the shooting, even though it's a pain doing it. Many students start shoots taking copious notes, only to drop the process as it gets complicated—you have to resist this urge. Your camera and sound notes are only the beginning of the peeling-away that occurs in postproduction.

Two kinds of editors

There are essentially two kinds of editors. In the first category are those who believe you can impose a rhythm on the material. Those in the second category think the rhythm's already there when you shoot it; they believe that all you have to do as an editor is find what that timing is, then your job is to take away everything that doesn't need to be there. I'm both kinds.

Sometimes you'll have had trouble finding the truth of the scene during shooting. The actors were a little off, the script could have used more work, your directing was weak on that particular day. You eased up. You didn't keep the focus that was needed during the shoot. It's understandable. Nobody can be on form all the time, especially on a long shoot, as the schedule progresses and crew members get tired. This happens to the actors in particular. Emotional exhaustion is part of the process. When that happens,

it becomes your job as the director to infuse the material with life during the editing process. You have to impose on it some kind of form that perhaps is hinted at but is not quite there from the shoot. When this happens, you just hope that you have enough there to make it work—and you usually do.

Film or digital?

Some film purists believe that students need to learn filmmaking by working on film. In other words, they should leave digital cameras till much later. Film is harder to shoot and more expensive, so discipline becomes an important aspect of the shoot—you shoot what you need, as you can't really afford to shoot much more. That gives you fewer choices when it comes time to edit.

While I believe discipline is key and should be stressed, I think that insisting on keeping students on film for a long time is archaic. The wisdom that dictates that students should use only film for a while has some of its roots in the belief that old school is better. This holds that there's a benefit from learning in this fashion that's intrinsically missing from teaching using only modern equipment, and that we've lost something precious as cameras have become easier to use.

So far as I'm concerned, there is no virtue in this nostalgic view. Sometimes old school is not better and technology does improve things. And if we do lose something, then there it is—it's lost. Better to move forward.

nostalgic

In any case, shooting film has become an archaic method of working, reserved for directors who prefer the vintage look that only celluloid can provide. It is indeed beautiful, but so is the footage you can get with some of the modern cameras. As Francis Ford Coppola says, "Cinema itself is technology." Embrace what's new, and work with whatever technology is best for you.

Filmmaking is a rogue art form anyway. It doesn't subscribe to any idealistic view of itself. Making movies is a need to say something and to say it in any way you can. If you have to shoot your movie with your phone, then do so. Whatever it takes. Tell your story. In fact, students going into film school these days have been making movies with their phones and their computers from a very young age. No doubt in another 20 years it'll be completely different. Film is a tool to achieve something else—it's not a means in itself.

Maximize your footage
Sometimes you do have to impose order on things. In those cases, having more footage is better than having less, because it gives you more options. I encourage my students to give themselves some choices when they shoot. Shoot as much as time permits. It won't be all that much anyway, because time constraints will rein you in. It's better to have it and not need it, than to need it and not have it.

No one gets it right the first time—we have to try and try again. One of the most brutal discoveries you'll make as a filmmaker is that your ideas are often not good enough at first. This is not easy to accept. We come up with a lot of terrible ideas and need time to weed out some of them. You evolve and learn as you work. The ideas you had at the beginning of making the movie may change in the process of

making it, which is a good thing. If they don't, then the process didn't affect you at all, and if that's the case, how can you hope that it'll influence others?

So you shoot a scene. In it, the character walks into the bathroom and brushes his teeth while looking out the window. Fabulous. More compelling scenes have rarely been shot.

You do the whole thing in one take. When you shoot it, you think, perfect. The actor was activated, he was looking out the window, and he was thinking about what he was going to do next. Even in the performance you could see he was reminiscing about something that had happened between him and another character. A fabulous acting moment. You think, "I have it. Let's move on."

Wrong. Give yourself options. Shoot the scene from a different angle, using some other shot. Perhaps a close-up so we can see what's going on with the actor. Remember, if you don't show us the face, we can't really tell what's going on. Maybe you should do a shot of what he's seeing out the window, or maybe an insert of him rinsing the toothbrush.

This is called **shooting coverage**. You cover the scene using other shots, so that you can cut to those shots if you need to. (Of course, a scene where the character is brushing his teeth can probably be shot easily and effectively with only one shot. But I'm trying to make a point.)

What seems perfect on the day of the shoot may not seem quite so perfect later. Months into the schedule, when you're cutting the footage, that long pause while the actor is thinking feels like the world is standing still. When you put the scene there, with the other edited scenes, it slows you down to a crawl. It turns out that the moment you thought was so powerful now seems like the most boring thing in the whole world.

"Give yourself options. Shoot the scene from a different angle, using some other shot."

From that wide shot of him brushing his teeth and looking out the window, cut to whatever it is he's looking at, perhaps some couple on the street, or a dog, or a plane taking off, whatever it is. Then cut back to the close-up and that moment of reminiscing. Boom. You just cut the timing of that scene to probably less than half. Cutting is used to compress time. But if you don't have choices to cut to, then you're stuck with that long, drawn-out shot. Don't let that happen.

You impose rhythm and order on what's going on. This is a good method, no doubt, but I believe the other way is better: when you find the rhythm that's already there. If you've done your job right—honing your writing, and directing your actors so that they hit their moments while you are shooting—then the timing already exists. All you have to do is take away all the parts that are not truthful.

Bruce Lee said, "It's not daily increase but daily decrease—hack away the unessential." Just like a sculptor taking away all the pieces of stone or wood that are not the statue, the editor takes away everything that is not true, to reveal the beauty of what's inside.

We don't always get it right the first time, and in those cases you get another chance at making it good; you get to perform corrective surgery and impose order on something that's chaotic. At other times, you've hit all the marks you needed to hit, and now your job is to separate the wheat from the chaff. Both methods are valid and should be practiced.

Balancing act

Filmmaking is finding a balance between order and chaos. Sometimes you lean in one direction, and other times the opposite way. This balancing act is the essence of what you'll do.

If everything is under control, then you will not be changed by the process of making your film, and if you don't change, the material won't either. Making a film knowing all the answers will inevitably make for work that lacks life and immediacy.

On the other hand, if you don't impose order on the chaos of creative thinking, then you'll never be able to maintain a narrative, and you need that narrative to reach the audience. Remember that there are things the audience is expecting, such as a narrative. Deny them those elements at your own peril.

Allow your work to change you as you proceed. In this way, you'll be surprised by the outcome. The film is there for you to answer some questions you don't have answers to. As those answers reveal themselves to you, they will emerge for the audience as well.

outcome

Author Note

Shorter, stronger, more concise. Print this little motto onto a piece of paper and tape it to your computer monitor.

Shorter, stronger, more concise

I worked with a great producer in Los Angeles who would use the phrase "shorter, stronger, more concise" constantly. She used it while we were writing, while we shot, and certainly while we were editing.

I don't know how many times I've gone into the editing room and one of my students has told me, "I can't cut any more out of my film. It's as tight as it can be." Nonsense. In my ten years as a filmmaking instructor, I've never encountered a cut of a film that couldn't be made tighter and more effective.

When approaching a scene, ask yourself how late you can go into it while still maintaining the integrity of the story, and how soon you can get out. Come into each scene as late as you can, while the audience can still understand what's going on, and get out as soon as the important moment happens. Don't linger. The Romans called this *In medias res*, which means "in the middle of things"—that's where you should start the action.

The audience is smart. There's a lot they don't need to see to understand. Give them the juicy parts, and don't waste your time with preliminaries. If they wanted the long, drawn-out reality of life, they would watch their own existence on camera. But they didn't come to the theater to see their lives. So make sure you use "movie time," which means, "Show me only what you need to show me." The audience will infer the rest.

effective

Let's set up a scene: A couple meets at a busy restaurant. They sit down, they greet. One of them starts to talk about their day and the other relates a bit of bad news. The wife says, "I've been having an affair with your brother for the last six months." Then the husband starts to ask how this happened, how could they do this, etc, etc.

The scene is two pages long—let's cut it down. Do you really need the greeting? Haven't we met these people earlier in the film? Do we really need to hear them say "Hi" to one another? Perhaps we cut to them already sitting at the restaurant. The husband starts talking about his day and then the wife gives him the bit of bad news. And for that matter, do we need all the whining that happens after the bad news? Couldn't we jump right into the consequences of what's going on?

So what we end up with is a couple at a restaurant and the wife saying, "I've been having an affair with your brother for the last six months." Then the look from the husband. Then back to the wife. They don't say anything else. Finally, we cut to the husband moving out of the house a few days later.

Doesn't that feel better? You understood the story, right? And it's more dynamic and agile.

There is such a thing as overdoing this and you can get to a point where your story becomes a collection of staccato moments that don't allow the audience time to absorb what's going on. My suggestion is go to that edge and then walk yourself back a few steps.

I like to err on the side of tighter, rather than on the side of too drawn out. But you're going to have to use your own sense of timing on this.

A short film should feel like a song by the Beatles: catchy, entertaining, with no time to linger. For me, the capital sin in moviemaking is to bore the audience. Please, please, please, don't bore me. I'd rather play catch up than be ahead of the story any day.

In the process of producing any work of art, there are elements that will be dear to your heart. We try to keep them because they're special to us, but ultimately they're harming the work. If you're holding on to something in your work—a shot, a scene, a camera move, an element of production design, anything—the fact that you're attached to it probably indicates that the reason for its being there has nothing to do with the story.

CASE STUDY: WALTER MURCH

Walter Murch is one of the premier film editors and sound designers in the industry. You can see his work in *Tomorrowland, The Wolfman, Jarhead, Cold Mountain, The English Patient, The Godfather Parts I and III*, and much more. He's won three Academy Awards. When he's editing, he doesn't like to go on set or know anything about how the production went. He doesn't meet the actors. That way, when he edits the movie, he won't be biased and can judge how the pieces of the movie fit within the edit. He needs to be able to cut that scene mercilessly. When editing, he pastes a color print of the opening frame of every shot on the wall, so the room is covered with them.

Get organized

Editing a movie can be overwhelming. Average **shooting ratios** are ten to one. That means that for every minute of film you end up with, you've probably shot ten times as much. Sometimes it's even more. In some cases, those numbers can be extreme, if you're the type of director who likes to do a lot of takes, or the material you're doing requires you to shoot a lot, like action sequences. Or perhaps you're editing a documentary and there's plenty of footage that was shot in the "running and gunning" style. In those instances, you may have hours' worth of material, sometimes a month's worth, sometimes years' worth.

That in itself is reason enough to get organized. This is when **camera and sound notes** (logs that the script supervisor and sound mixer keep concurrently as the shoot goes on) come in handy. If you have ten takes of the same shot, there's no need to sync all ten. Take the two you like the most, which have the best performances. Do that with every shot and then cut the film together with those.

Only if you run into problems of continuity do you go back to your original bunch of takes and perhaps sync some others. What that means is that sometimes there are differences in continuity that prevent you from cutting two takes together, two takes that you would otherwise use. For example, the actor may not have been holding the mug exactly the same way in both takes, or he didn't drink the coffee at precisely the same time. When that happens, you may have to go back to the original group of takes to find something that matches. Otherwise, don't kill yourself syncing everything.

As a director, you should qualify each take by telling the script supervisor if it was poor, good, or exactly what you wanted. In the old days a director would say to print that take. Not every bit of negative was developed, only the takes the director wanted. So it pays to know the takes that you liked and have good sound. That way you're not doing unnecessary work.

Once you have all your material in your editing system, whatever that system might be, on your first run through it, it's best to label each shot with some kind of information that'll help you remember what's on that clip. That way you know that a particular take is the one that has the actor doing that thing you wanted, or the footage of the kids running on the street, or the take with the airplane flying by. The trick is to make the title descriptive and yet short enough for it to be practical.

When you see something on a clip, assume you will not see that clip again until you need it for cutting. If you don't label it the first time you see it, you'll have to find it again when you need it. Try that when you have years' worth of footage.

Another trick is to have the slate in front of the camera *before* you roll. If you're diligent about this while shooting, then when you put all your clips into your editing program, that thumbnail on the computer screen will have a picture of the slate on the first frame. It makes it a lot easier to identify each shot.

syncing

I then divide the shots into folders identifying each scene. Some editors like to place these folders in even larger ones corresponding to sequences or acts. The more organized you get, the easier it is to do a job that has plenty of complexity to it already. Get yourself set before you start cutting.

Another thing I like to do is get all my music and sound effects into the program before I start to cut. There's nothing worse than having to stop your creative flow to go find a piece of music, convert it to specifications, and then import it into your project. It's much better when everything you need is at your fingertips.

Your **DIT** (digital imaging technician) should make two copies of your drive as the shoot progresses—don't put everything on just one drive. Hard drives are

notorious for burning out or crashing. Make copies and make sure you update the copies of the project files as you continue to work.

It's difficult for students to understand the importance of getting organized. They start working on small projects with minimal shots or takes, so when they start to edit, they can keep in their head where everything is. But as projects grow, the amount of footage will quickly become unmanageable. I've seen documentaries with editors sorting through years' worth of footage, because that's how long a filmmaker has been working on something.

I was an assistant editor for commercials when I first moved to Los Angeles. All that means is that you come in, sometimes late at night, and organize the footage for the actual editor, who will arrive in the morning, ready to get to work. As assistant editor, you're the one who does the jobs like syncing sound to picture, putting clips into folders, and getting the music and sound effects ready. The assistant editor position is one of the entryways into the business. If you do a good job, it'll be no time before you are being asked to do some cutting. Soon you'll have an editing position of your own.

Timing, timing, timing

After you've got organized, next comes the rough assembly, or what is called the **rough cut**. For a director who has the luxury of working with an editor, this might be the time to take a break from the material and try to gain some perspective. If you've been working on a feature from development till the end of principal photography, you've probably spent four months to a year working on the project. This is a good opportunity to get away from the work for at least a week, to refresh your system for the work that lies ahead.

During this time the editor will produce an **assembly cut** (a rough draft of the cut) of the material. Basically, they'll be putting together the pieces roughly where they need to be. There will be no refining of the cut at all at this stage. Then, after that week off, you can come back and start giving your editor notes on the cut.

If you're the one who'll be cutting the film, then I suggest you still give yourself at least a few days off. It will allow time for you to gain some distance from the shoot before you have to start cutting. One of your classmates could sync your project for you and organize the footage, then you could do the same for them sometime.

As you start to dig into the material and correct the initial rough assembly, what you're looking for is for the material to "sing," when the cut is at its optimal level of timing—things are just as long or as short as they need to be. This will vary from project to project, of course. But here is where we go back to finding the truth in the performance.

CASE STUDY: *JAWS* (AGAIN)

I keep going back to this movie, because it's one of the masterpieces of cinema. *Jaws* was the first blockbuster. Lines at the ticket booths went around the block, hence the term "blockbuster." When the editor, Verna Fields, showed Spielberg her cut of the movie, he wanted more footage of the shark. But Fields assured him that she had used as much and as little footage as she could for the desired effect. In some instances she only had a few frames of shark when the mechanical beast didn't look sluggish and unconvincing. They tried some of the shots with the extra frames Spielberg wanted and, of course, Fields had been right. The way she had cut those shots was the only way they could have been cut.

cutting

A good editor will start to trim the takes by taking out the actors' moments that are not truthful, leaving only the pieces that hit the notes right on the nose. In this way, the hidden timing of the piece will emerge. This is a very organic process.

There are editors who have a natural sense of this timing. Others are not as fortunate. Once you find a person who can do this well, hold on to them. Keep working with them, because they'll learn your own sense of timing and that will make the process a lot easier. That's why you see directors working with the same editors over and over again.

When you're cutting, take into consideration everything that will be seen or heard: when the music comes in, when a title dissolves into the screen, when a shot goes to black, when an actor's eyes shift. Everything becomes part of the overall timing of the movie and should be taken into consideration.

When you've reached the optimal timing, you'll know it: The piece will have a life of its own. This change might take place from one moment to another. You're working away on something that feels okay but not great. Then you adjust a cut and, all of a sudden, the movie's there. It sings.

At that moment, it becomes apparent how important timing really is, revealing itself as a component of cinematic language that's as strong as contrast or the composition of the shot. Timing tells the story just as much as anything else. When you come into a scene, when you leave, when the music swells, and countless other choices you'll have to make all dictate how efficient the movie will be in communicating the emotional life of the work. All at once, it happens. One moment you're cutting and the next you can't think of the piece being cut in any other way. It's movie magic.

Don't be technologically challenged!

Learn your software. The more skills you have as a filmmaker, the more opportunities you'll have for employment. Once you're inside a company, it becomes natural for you to move up. Just make sure your work is always on point.

It doesn't really matter what software you use—Adobe Premier, Apple's Final Cut Pro, Avid, DaVinci Resolve, or any of the half-dozen other programs out there. Avid has for many years been the industry standard, but it doesn't matter what technology you use, as long as you apply the principles we've been discussing.

software

The more familiar you become with the editing software, the more creative you can be. In one project I did with my students, I wanted to add some special effects to a horror movie I was shooting, but I didn't have the budget to add anything that would cost any money. It was my knowledge of the editing system that came to my rescue.

I used a composite shot to create the illusion of a ghost walking on a wall. First, I shot what we call the **plate**, done with actors in the foreground and space enough to insert my FX shot. Next, I shot the ghost on a white floor, at the same angle that the camera would be looking at it if it had been crawling on the wall. Then I blended the two shots together. The shot cost no money at all and went a long way toward selling the premise of the film. To this day I still use tricks like those. When you're working on a budget, knowledge becomes the best friend of creativity.

Here's the same technique used in two projects. That original film I did with my students is on the left and a current project is on the right.

A movie's finishing school

After **picture lock** (when the cut is finished
and approved), it's time for sound design, color
correction, and color grading. It is also time for any
additional dialogue recordings that might be needed,
along with **Foley**, which refers to the reproduction
of all sound that's heard in the movie.

That's right, all the sounds you hear in a movie were
reproduced in a studio. Our minds are accustomed to
the levels of this reproduced sound, so the real sound
that might have been recorded while the performance
was taking place no longer seems real to us. We have
to have every sound manufactured. And when I say
every sound, I mean every single one, from people
touching their clothes, to footsteps going down an
alley, to gunshots, to forks going into mouths and
hitting teeth. All of this is done in postproduction.

These finishing touches are what ultimately sell
the movie to the audience, because they make it
seem more real. The audience will forgive mistakes
in the recording of the image—many times they'll
attribute them to a stylistic choice. But errors in the
recording of the sound, especially when it comes to

quality, will immediately bump the audience out of their suspension of disbelief and will categorize the moviemakers as amateurs.

My advice to young filmmakers in this respect is to hire a pro. Unless you've decided to become an image technician or a sound engineer, there's going to be somebody out there that will be able to do it better than you.

Color correction and **color grading** refer to the manipulation of the intensity and quality of the colors of the film, as well as the controlling of the blacks and highlights. We're highlighting what we want to highlight and taking down what we don't really want to see so well. We're crushing the blacks so that they appear menacing and ominous on screen, or highlighting the light coming from a window to make it look like the characters are in heaven. We're also refining the color palette of the film, as if we were giving an oil painting the last few strokes of the brush to bring forth the important elements of the picture.

The things you can do with the software we have today are amazing. My students learn to use the DaVinci Resolve. You can manipulate light sources, highlight them, and make them move with an actor's face. It really does give new meaning to the phrase "fix it in post."

CASE STUDY: *THE MATRIX*
In 1999 the Wachowskis wanted a special
effect that would convey the sense of time
standing still for their film *The Matrix*. They
wanted the camera to rotate 180 degrees
around a subject suspended in midair while
bullets whistled by, but it was impossible to
move the camera fast enough. The solution
they came up with, with John Gaeta at Manex
Visual Effects, was to place stills cameras
around the subject. Each took one frame, and
when all the frames had been put together,
the effect approached a frame frequency
of 12,000 per second (compared with 24
per second from a movie camera). While
making a movie about technology turning
against humanity, the Wachowskis had used
filmmaking technology to take the art form to
another level. They called it bullet time.

In fact, "fix it in post" has become a running joke in the filmmaking business. A lazy director would say it when they didn't want to spend the time or effort or money to do it right while shooting. Of course, most problems that can arise from the shoot are not fixable in post, although today's sophisticated computer programs mean that the gap between what's doable and what's not is diminishing. Soon you will be able to say "fix it in post" and it won't be a joke anymore.

Some directors like to manipulate the frame more than others. Directors such as David Fincher go as far as moving or removing buildings in a city skyline shot because he doesn't like the position of the structures. With the development of more and more powerful CGI programs and computers, there is really no limit to what we can do.

Stanley Kubrick once said, "If it can be written or thought, it can be filmed." I think he meant that you could find a creative way to shoot it, as he did very well in movies like *2001: A Space Odyssey*. But today that has become almost a literal statement.

Programs will continue to evolve and improve. Stay abreast of the new technology coming out, because film is technology. Use all the tools at your disposal to tell a story. And when encountering a discipline that's not your strong suit, find an expert who will bring your film to the next level. A director needs a team to make their vision come alive, so get the best team you can.

There is a distinct pleasure in listening to your film for the first time after it comes back from the sound designer. It's like a completely different movie. This is also true after it has been color corrected. You sit there and wonder, "Wow, who made this? It really looks professional." It's a testament to what a skilled technician can do to make the illusion come alive.

technology

DIRECTING: WHAT IS IT?

A director translates a concept, a dream, a story into executable shots. Yes, you need a lot of hard and soft skills to make that happen, but essentially you're turning a vision into shots that can be put together so the vision can be shared with an audience.

Directing is the reverse engineering of a dream. The concept starts out as an image in your head—a particular scene that has activated your imagination. Whatever it is that you see in this story is contained in that moment, and the story becomes a frame for it to come through.

The screenwriter and filmmaker Tony Gilroy said that when he was tasked with writing an adaptation of *The Bourne Identity* book, what struck him was the scene in which Jason Bourne is in a diner with a woman who's helping him out. Bourne doesn't know who he is but he can remember certain information and skills, though he doesn't know how. The scene captured Gilroy's imagination, so he crafted his story around this one concept.

So that's how you start. You have a concept that gets your imaginative engine revving and you craft a story around it. Because you understand how humans tell stories, you give it a beginning, a middle, and an end. You try to generate empathy toward your protagonist. You make every scene part of this plot by having the character make a decision in order to move forward. Or perhaps you move the story by unfolding a revelation. Either way, through conflict you reach the climactic scene when the character has to make the biggest decision of the film.

Fantastic, you have your story. But remember that a script is only a blueprint for something else. You still have to make a film. So you have to take these scenes and translate them into things you can do.

The building blocks of a script are words, scenes, paragraphs of description, dialogue. The building blocks of a movie are shots. So you convert each scene into executable shots. Each shot hopefully communicates something and is aesthetically pleasing.

What you're doing is imposing order on chaos. A director becomes a translation device between the worlds of chaos, of imagination, and of order and understanding. You take matter that's dreamlike and you turn it into something more solid—a shot that we can light and rehearse, and in which we can place actors in front of a lens. The actors pretend to do something and we record it so that we can combine it with other shots and create the illusion of life. It can blow your mind when you think about it.

Making a movie is rather like magic: It's a long, complex spell. If you do it right, it creates life, in the form of characters who didn't previously exist. You see them live their lives—and not just regular lives but dramatic stories designed to enlighten. When done well, filmmaking is the ultimate creative act. From the void, through word and image, you bring forth life, or at least the illusion of it.

HOW I BECAME A DIRECTOR

When I was 18, I went to New York to become an actor. While at NYU and also after graduating, I did some production work, learning to operate a control booth and work with cameras and sound recording equipment, but I was still focused on acting. Sometimes, though, as I was working on a shoot, I could tell that the people making the movie had no idea what they were doing. I finally decided I could do it better, so I asked a friend who had been a film student to teach me to make a movie. It took him about half an hour to give me the basics and recommend a few books. That was it—I was a director, and after a few months I made my first film.

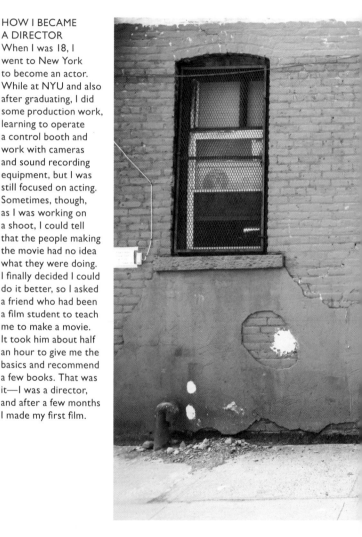

**"An artist
wants to know
they're part of
something bigger
than themselves."**

How to lead

Directors are leaders, and leaders are people who can ask real questions of themselves and be truly interested in finding out what the answers might be. They do not know all the answers. In order to be a leader you have to go into the unknown and ask questions you don't know the answers to, then do your best to respond anyway. The solution is in the doing. There's a distinct possibility that you won't actually like the answers, but that's the first step toward becoming a leader. You need to be able to ask yourself real questions and accept the challenges of the answers that you know deep down are the correct ones.

A director *has* to be a leader—everybody in the crew and cast is looking to take their cues from you. They want to know that what they're doing is worth it, and I'm not talking about financial compensation. Worth or purpose is what drives true artists. The cast and crew are looking to you to provide that, and it's the most important thing you'll give them. A crew with a clear purpose will go out of their way and beyond their pay rate to get it for you. An artist wants to know they're part of something bigger than themselves.

Preparation, preparation, preparation

I insist that my students prepare for their shoots. I have them make a shot list, a storyboard, and a floor plan for every scene. Some take to it like a fish to water, while others hate it, but it's important to prepare for all the things that can go wrong during production. That's just part of the filmmaker's credo.

Nothing really goes according to plan—in which case, wouldn't it just be better if you just were to wing it when you get to set? Unequivocally, *no*. The more you spend time thinking about a shoot, and in particular each shot, the better you'll be at solving the inevitable problems that will arise on set, even if it means changing the plan. Time you spend working on the storyboards is time you spend thinking about what you're going to do. Thinking is good! Go back to asking yourself those hard questions and searching hard for the answers.

Spend time planning your shots and, if nothing else, you'll become an expert at your own material. By the time you get to the shoot you'll know exactly why and how you're going to do each shot. Then when the members of the crew or the cast ask you, you'll have a fabulous explanation for your actions.

I encourage my students to draw their storyboards. Some can only manage stick figures, but that's absolutely okay, as long as they spend time doing them.

If you have access to the location, a great way to storyboard is to take a camera with a zoom lens on location along with some actors, or at least some warm bodies, and take pictures of every shot you're planning on doing. Have your DP and your AD with you and you can create the shot list as you go along. You'll be able to get a sense of the space and also to figure out what lens you'll use for each shot. There are phone apps that will change the length of the lens on your camera phone so that you can see what a 16mm lens would look like as opposed to an 85, or a 35, or a 50. In fact, those are probably the four lenses you'll get with a basic package of prime (non-zoom) lenses.

I encourage my students to draw their floor plans as well, or to use an app like Shot Designer, which lets you create sets and place characters and cameras, moving them around the screen like chess pieces.

Dark and Turns and draws

The other benefit of storyboarding and floor planning is that it'll be easier for the crew to understand what needs to happen. They'll have an illustration of what the shot looks like, a map of where the camera and the lights go, and the sequence in which to film it.

You can take the shot list, cut it into strips, and create a board on set. Simply paste the strips to cardboard, a wall, or the inside of a door, and set the times scheduled to do each shot next to them. As you complete each shot, you can cross it off or take it off the board. It becomes a central place for the crew and the actors to gather and see what comes next and also helps you stay honest with the schedule.

Always do a board. I don't know how many times I've had students tell me that they forgot to do a shot they wanted because they had no way of tracking what had been done.

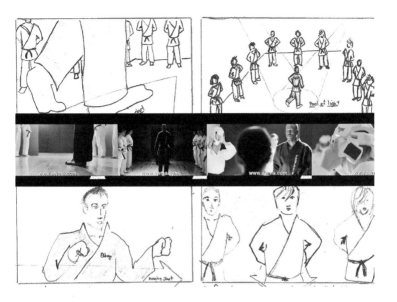

Author Note
Here are a couple of my own storyboards, together with the corresponding shots.

"In your choices lies your talent"

Stella Adler used to tell her acting students, "In your choices lies your talent," and my teacher, who had studied with her, also quoted it to us in class. He used to say it was an incredibly deep statement, though I found it hard to see that at the time. Filmmaking, in many respects, is the art of making choices. You make choices every step of the way: in the material you decide to tackle, the people you'll work with, the locations you'll shoot in, what shots to do, how you'll shoot them, what props to use, what colors, how much time to spend on a sequence, and endless other decisions. My understanding of Adler's statement now has to do with the fact that talent is not some preordained thing that lives within you and can't be affected by what's around you. Instead, talent is dependent on the amount of focus we give it. The more energy we pour into it, the more it evolves. Talent develops from the choices you make every day:

- Did you decide to work or to go out and party?
- Did you decide to give up or continue to try to crack that problem you have with the script?
- Did you decide to get up at 5am to work on your script or did you sleep a few more hours?
- Did you decide to cast the actor who was almost right or did you hold out to find the perfect person?
- Did you decide to ease up and not pay attention to a shot or did you assume responsibility for every frame in your film?

In your choices lies your talent. That means that your ability to do good work, to use your instrument at the peak of its output, is dependent not on something you can't control, but on your work ethic and your effort and your choices.

Life itself is making choices. Don't disregard any of them as being inconsequential—certainly not while you're making a film.

CASE STUDY: THE STAR GATE SEQUENCE

One of the many choices you make as a director is whom you're going to work with and how much you'll let them run with their own notions and ideas for the work. When Stanley Kubrick was shooting *2001: A Space Odyssey*, he needed a sequence that would convey traveling from one dimension to another. This couldn't be shot by any means known at the time. He had to come up with an entire visual concept that would communicate the event to the audience, *and* a way of getting it on film.

Kubrick tasked special-effects artist Doug Trumbull, then aged just 23, with coming up with an idea. Trumbull experimented with several methods and finally decided on a new form of streak photography. Streak photography is when you open the shutter of the camera for a prolonged period of time and the subject is moving. This gives you that familiar effect of the lights of cars on a freeway turning into bars of light in the night.

Trumbull did this on a three-dimensional frame and with a camera that had been stripped of its shutter. He moved neon tubes of light in front of the lens, turning them on and off and moving them in different patterns, keeping the camera running the whole time. Each frame of the sequence took five minutes to shoot.

Trumbull had invented the entire concept of the image and then created a way to shoot it, and Kubrick had trusted another artist to help him. He knew how much freedom and responsibility to give Trumbull, who took ownership of the sequence and poured his heart and soul into making it great. The result is one of the most innovative and aesthetically cinematic sequences in movie history.

Communication is key

A director needs to learn to become a great communicator. You can't make your movie on your own—you're going to have to hire others to help you. In order for their work to fit into the concept of your film, you'll have to communicate what you want to them. Sometimes you'll be explaining concepts that are ambiguous and not fully formed in your own head. This is not easy, especially as you have to do it before you make the film.

Start by telling them what brought you to the material in the first place, what inspires you about it. Then, as concisely as possible, try to explain what you want to achieve.

How much does it take?

One of my teachers in college used to put his hand on your shoulder while you were seated and then ask you to get up. As you tried to do so, he would put some pressure on your shoulder to make it harder. He didn't make it impossible, just a little bit more difficult. After you had struggled your way up, he would ask, "How much did it take?" Students would invariably give an assortment of answers, all of them wrong, until he finally answered it himself: "It takes as much as it takes."

At first it seemed like a ridiculous answer—*of course* it takes as much as it takes. But upon closer inspection I realized that it's not because we don't know it, but because we haven't accepted its implications. We know, but we haven't accepted it yet. This is one of the cruxes of human existence. Most of what we need, in order to do whatever it is we want to do, we already know, or at least we would if we dared to ask the right questions. But do we dare?

pressure

committed

We form an idea of how much we'll need to do to get something. This is a dangerous habit, because it accustoms us to thinking we know what it should take to get something done. In fact, there is no such thing as too much work for something we want. If we truly do want it, we should be prepared to do whatever it takes to get it done. And that will usually be a lot more than we imagined.

I run into this problem with my students all the time. I'm teaching an acting for film class, my students come in to do a scene, and they don't know their lines. They studied them, they think they know them, but when the camera starts to roll their minds go blank. They don't really know them. Some have even tried to learn their lines on the morning of the class.

The world doesn't conform to you—it is indifferent to what you think. You have to deal with whatever's there. We don't get to decide what's fair and what's not. And besides, "fair" is a made-up word. It exists only in our minds. What we do get to decide is how much we are willing to do. So, if we set ourselves a limit, then we'll reach that boundary and give up instead of breaking through. How much does it take? As much as it takes.

If you learn this one lesson in life, you will be better prepared to deal with any situation—from applying to college, to talking to your kids, to finishing that dissertation you've been working on for the last five years. I cannot stress enough how important this really is.

Tell yourself you're prepared to do whatever it takes to achieve your goals, and you're really prepared to go there, then you will keep going until you get what you want. There's no trick to achieving your goals. There's only the work you're willing to put in.

The problem with Plan B

The problem is that we say we are game to do whatever it takes but that comes with an expiration date. We are not *really* committed. We will do as much as we think is necessary but not more. At some point, we start thinking we shouldn't have to do this much, then we quit and move on to Plan B.

Forget Plan B. It is the reason a lot of people are unhappy. They settle for the option that's not so difficult. If we have a plan B, we will find a reason to go there. We always do. Just like water running downhill, we are designed to follow the path of least resistance. The problem is that what we truly want also comes packed with opposing forces. We must navigate those forces.

Having an escape hatch has one big drawback: If we have a way out, we'll take it. And if we set ourselves a limit, we'll reach it.

DON'T GIVE UP

When I started working at ABC News, right out of college, a colleague for some reason decided she didn't want me working there and did all she could to get me to quit. The job was hard anyway but she made it harder. It felt like everyone was waiting for me to screw up. I called my father and told him I planned to quit, as it wasn't worth it. He wrote to me saying that sometimes we have to do things we don't want to, for the sake of our own growth. I stayed because of that letter. The amount of growing I did by struggling through that year was immeasurable—I came out stronger and smarter, and learned self-reliance and self-respect. I went on to win an Emmy and a Peabody award at that job.

The value of adversity

Adversity brings out the best in human beings. It brings out the worst sometimes, but it also brings out the best. Don't be afraid of adversity. Embrace it; become friends with it. You'll do your best work when confronted by it.

> "Filmmaking isn't sprinting, it's running a marathon. In fact, it's running a marathon every time you do a film."

It is said that when the Spanish conquistador Hernán Cortés reached the New World, he burned his ships. That was how he kept his soldiers motivated—they had no way of escape. They had to win or die. We have to assume the same level of commitment to what we want in life.

motivated

My students often ask me if I think they should be doing what they're doing, if they've made the right choice. What they really want is validation, because they are pretty close to giving up. They've encountered some opposition and so they are already thinking, "Maybe I chose wrong and I should go back home and study law and then pursue a career in filmmaking on the side." As if that were possible. I respond the same way whenever I'm asked this. "Is this what you want to do for the rest of your life?" Invariably they answer yes. That's a lie but that's usually what they answer.

Then I say, "So what does it matter what I think or what anybody else thinks of your choices? What does it matter how long it takes? If you've decided this is what you're going to do for the rest of your life, then relax and sit back. It's going to be a long ride."

Filmmaking isn't sprinting, it's running a marathon. In fact, it's running a marathon every time you do a film. That goes for being a writer, an actor, a musician, a painter, and all sorts of other artistic pursuits. How much does it take? As much as it takes!

When I was at NYU and I got up to perform during one of my first acting classes, my teacher said to me I sounded like Ricky Ricardo and that I should get off the stage. I was offended.

First, I didn't know who Ricky Ricardo was. And, second, didn't he know that I spoke two languages? Didn't he know that I sounded the way I sounded because Spanish was my first language? Didn't he know to ignore my accent and look at the deeper aspects of my performance? That my talent was worth overlooking all of these other misgivings and he should know that and he shouldn't bother me with such a trivial thing as the way I sounded?

Actually, my teacher was trying to get me into the real world rather than the world I had in my head. He was trying to make me understand that people out there don't care that English is not your first language. If you sound like that, you will be limited in the roles you will be offered. As a beginning actor you want to keep your options as open as possible.

I can hear you asking, "What about Antonio Banderas and Javier Bardem and Penélope Cruz and Sofía Vergara and Marion Cotillard?" First of all, those are five out of millions of actors trying to make it into Hollywood. You can't hang your hopes on the luck and the circumstances they experienced.

This is not about whether you have an accent or not, or whether that makes you a good actor or not. Good or bad has nothing to do with this. And accents are beautiful things that should be cherished. No, this is about self-control, self-discipline, and effort. This has to do with what it takes to achieve something and training your body to do it, no matter what.

After my teacher called me Ricky Ricardo, I resolved to be the best actor in his class. We were going to work on Shakespeare, so I bought a tape of an American play and listened obsessively on my headphones to the actors performing it. I paid attention to the way I talked. I bought accent-reduction tapes. I bought books. When I was done with that American play, I moved on to *King Lear*. I think I memorized every line of the play at some point—I knew all the parts. I listened and I imitated the way they spoke. In other words, I applied myself to the problem and I did whatever it took to solve it. I didn't care if I never listened to anything else on my headphones ever again.

It took me a couple of years, but when I was done, I was the best Shakespearean actor in the class.

Not only that, but I could walk into an audition and the casting director could not tell that I was Puerto Rican. They couldn't place me at all. I could fool native English speakers. It's one of the hardest things I've ever done. It was also a hundred percent worth it. And here's the kicker: I can always go back to my natural accent. It's in me; it's who I am. What I did wasn't to get rid of it, but to learn a skill.

Just keep going

That experience taught me a much more valuable lesson than just how to speak with a standard American accent. It was the fact that I had to be willing to do whatever it took to achieve something. What I had initially thought it would take wasn't enough; I had to go farther. The way you know you've done all you really can do is when you've achieved what you wanted. If you haven't achieved it, then you haven't done enough. It's not about fair or not fair. It's not about your idea of what you're willing to do. It's about what it is.

Early in my career as a filmmaker, I worked with a producer who used to love the phrase, "It is what it is." She was willing to do whatever it took to get something done. More so, in fact, as she understood that situations change.

I love that line from the movie *Invictus*, where Matt Damon, playing François Pienaar, the captain of the South African rugby team, tells Morgan Freeman, playing Nelson Mandela, "The truth is, sir, you never play at a hundred percent, no matter what." That's right, there's always something.

That doesn't mean you don't fight injustice when you see it. But don't strap yourself down to a limit just because you've figured out in your head that's all it should take.

Your limits are only in your mind. When you let go of those, that's when life will seem to bend to your will. Until then it may feel unfair and as though other people have all the luck. Nonsense. Go out there and get it done.

Besides, we weren't put on this earth to have it easy and be happy, but to strive for a purpose. That's what we're built for. If it were easy, it wouldn't be worth doing.

ZEN AND THE ART OF FILMMAKING

A teacher of mine shared a metaphor for filmmaking that describes the process to perfection. Imagine you're producing a jigsaw puzzle. You take a picture, like the *Mona Lisa*, cut it into hundreds of pieces, and put them in a box. You give it to somebody and when they put the pieces together it looks like the *Mona Lisa*. Fantastic! However, in filmmaking we take a blank piece of cardboard and we cut that into pieces. Next, we take one of these and draw on it, then we take another and draw on that one. We draw on every piece and put them in a box, then when somebody puts them together, it has to look like the *Mona Lisa*. That's how it feels to make a movie.

Enjoy the journey

Filmmaking is taking what you imagine and breaking it down into executable shots: into characters' stories, sound effects, camera setups, scene beats, lighting schemes, costume choices, and on and on. It's an amazing job.

The only way to survive and be good at it is to concentrate on the process and not the result. A lot of people *say* this, but they don't understand what it *means*. It doesn't mean you don't care about the result—you do care.

"We take
imagination
and we break
it down into
doable steps."

What you need to do is fall in love with crafting each of the pieces. You have to find the reward in the steps, shot by shot. Fall in love with figuring out how to move the camera, how to direct an actor, how to sit down to write a scene. Fall in love with hanging the lights and rehearsing and taking focus marks for a shot. Fall in love with musing about a project while you're alone, walking down a long and crowded street at night. Fall in love with watching other filmmakers work, with making sure there's enough contrast in a shot, and with making that cut so perfect the audience doesn't really notice you've changed perspectives. Fall in love with watching other people get inspired by your work, and with that moment you get your movie back from the editor, the sound designer, or the color corrector and you watch it afresh.

For many years I worked with an Israeli editor, with whom I would drink scotch or tequila while watching the first assembly cut (when the editor puts things together for the first time and hasn't gone in to do any refining yet). I remember those moments of sharing the excitement with my editor more than I do the cuts themselves. The possibilities were endless.

We take imagination and we break it down into doable steps. Sometimes we don't reach the end, just like in life. That's not really a tragedy—it's just the way it is. But if we are concentrating so much on the end result that we forget to stop and enjoy what we're doing in the present, *that* is a tragedy.

Living in the moment
Eckhart Tolle, one of my favorite spiritual teachers, said, "But then you miss your whole life, which is never not now." Absolutely right.

Filmmaking is the same—it is always in the now. It must be. That's why scripts are written in the present tense. Even as we watch a film that we've completed, we're watching the film with our audience in the present. It's in the present for the actors acting it because that moment is frozen in time. The now of making the film mixes with the now of watching it. If we're lucky, it mixes with the now of generations to come and they get to live something they wouldn't get to live any other way.

The joy of escapism

We go to the movies to experience what we don't get in real life. Or sometimes we go to see from the outside exactly what's happening in our lives, because living it feels just too hard.

The author and screenwriter Robert McKee said, "We go to the movies to enter a new, fascinating world, to inhabit vicariously another human being… to live in a fictional reality that illuminates our daily reality." One of the benefits of the lights going down is to give you privacy, so that you can have that communion with the art form.

So when I go to the movies I don't want that man on the screen to have the same argument with his lover I have with mine. I want him to say and do the things I never dared. They tell us in life to guard our hearts, never get really angry, never let ourselves be caught out in the open. We go to the movies to experience the forbidden things.

The mark of the filmmaker

In order for the audience to enjoy what they're watching, for it to really resonate in their souls, it has to have the enjoyment of the filmmaker imprinted on it. All the great filmmakers have left their marks on their films.

One of those marks was love for the work. Love leaves the footprint of love, no matter what else happens. And no love ever happens without effort or without heartache.

There will come a time when you're on set and you've been working 14-hour days for six days straight and your back hurts. Your brain is refusing to work, you're

hot and sweaty and cranky, and everybody around you is in a bad mood. This is not a moment for despair—it's a moment of opportunity. It is the moment when you can and should inspire your crew. And it is the moment when you can decide whether this crazy art form is something you really want to do for the rest of your life. It's an opportunity to grow into the giant you are meant to be.

At that moment, when you can't give any more, when your body is asking you to quit and your mind is agreeing, you have a chance to transcend. If you've picked your material and your crew well, and if you've been true to yourself, that is the moment you've been waiting for. It is not something to be feared, but to be embraced. When exhaustion takes you, all you have left to operate with is heart. And that's the filmmaker's greatest weapon.

Embrace being miserable. As Steven Pressfield said (see page 39), it is the artist's natural state. It's where they should be, your place in the universe—because out of it comes our greatest gift.

When we're in the fight, the thing that scares us most is not the possibility of having to go to the wall to win. It is the necessity of having to go so many times *just* to survive. But in that struggle lies true greatness. In that struggle is when we touch God.

CASE STUDY: MIKE LEIGH

Mike Leigh is a British writer-director with a unique way of developing a project. He starts with no script. Instead, he gives the actors a premise for their encounters. He works with each in private for a while and then has them meet the other members of the cast as they would in real life, at the moment he feels their lives would intersect.

The script is developed from a series of improvisations and explorations into the characters and their relationships. After the actors have fleshed out the situations, Leigh writes the script out of the moments they have created together. What results is a film with an unwavering dedication to finding the truth of the situation and of the humans in it. Process above everything.

TWO

WHAT HAPPENS
AFTER FILM
SCHOOL?

What happens after film school?

You go on to create some content, of course. At least, that's the goal. There are many great jobs in this industry that are available to you after you've graduated from film school.

GETTING KNOWN

Some of the entry-level positions include such jobs as grip, production assistant, assistant editor, runner, driver, assistant camera, and associated director. These are all great jobs and are good ways to get into a crew (see page 67). Once you're in a crew, you'll work consistently with them and you'll move up in the ranks.

The best town to do this in is Los Angeles, because of the number of jobs available. There's more done in LA than anywhere else. Other good places for filmmaking jobs are New York and Atlanta. These are highly contested jobs and the numbers are limited. But the opportunities are there all the same, and the more skills you have, the more employable you become.

WHEN OPPORTUNITY KNOCKS
When I moved to LA in 2003, I had been a production assistant and an associate director for nine years in New York. My first job in LA was translating commercials from English to Spanish, and vice versa, for NBC.

One day I was in the office when an opportunity for a shoot came along. Our two cameramen were out on assignments, so I told the producer I'd do it. I knew how to operate a camera, but I wasn't familiar with the one they used here, a Canon XL2 3CCD. I took the camera case and left for location, about an hour away. When I got there and opened the case, the camera was in pieces. It had to be assembled, and

I had no idea how to do it. So I called a friend in New York, he talked me through it, and I assembled the camera and did the shoot.

When I got back to LA, the producer needed somebody to cut the material. I had learned Final Cut the year before, so I volunteered. A year later, I was a director of this company and had a crew of my own.

Speeding up the process

- Luck is opportunity meets preparation. Acquire marketable skills. The more you have, the more viable for jobs you become.
- If there's a possibility you can figure out on your own how to do what's required, just say yes to the job, and then work out how to do it.
- There's a lot of work out there as an assistant editor, an animator, a production assistant, or any of the thousands of other entry-level jobs in the industry. The trick is to go to one of the places where demand is high.
- Instead of looking for a job that already exists, create your own, especially if you want to start directing films as soon as possible. Don't wait for somebody to give you what you want—create it yourself.
- Go direct. Start small. Don't wait.

Connections

One of the hidden advantages of film school is that if you're diligent and dedicated, you acquire the one thing you can't do without when trying to make a movie: a crew.

Technology has gotten to the point that the equipment needed to make a film is readily available to everyone.

Yes, of course, some equipment is expensive and hard to come by. But you don't need the latest and greatest camera to get started—use whatever's available to you at the moment. Steven Soderbergh shot his last two films (*Unsane* and *High Flying Bird*) with an iPhone 7 Plus. He raved about the freedom it gave him to keep his actors in character and move from shot to shot with previously unheard-of speed.

So don't get preoccupied with the equipment you have. Remember that the most important thing is your story and how you tell it.

The people who make movies with you in school can be the same people that help you make your movies outside of school. If you've developed a relationship with some of your fellow students, those are the people who are the logical first choice to become your crew.

This really showcases the importance of being reliable and dedicated while you're doing your shoots in film school. If your classmates get to know you as somebody who's also inspiring and fun to work with, they're going to want to foster and continue that relationship. They can help you with their project and you can help them with theirs. You can do films, web series, music videos, documentaries—content of all kinds. The possibilities are endless.

And with the new avenues for distribution, especially the internet, you don't even have to wait for somebody to buy your show. You can put it online and start acquiring views. People have careers through their own channels on YouTube.

There's really nothing standing in your way. Gather your friends together and have a brainstorming session. Come up with some concepts and get started. No time like the present.

Monkey on your back

Because we work in a highly competitive business, an entire industry has sprung up out of the need to find work. It's an industry of seminars, self-help gurus, referral services, and the like. Sometimes they help you develop your work. Sometimes they workshop it and have readings in front of executives. Some services make promises about introducing you to top-tier executives. But beware of the easy fix. Whenever somebody promises something that sounds too good to be true, it usually is.

I'm not saying all these classes are bad. On the contrary, there are a lot of great teachers out there. One of the first seminars I took on scriptwriting was given by Robert McKee and it was absolutely fantastic. At the time of writing this book, he's still at it. And there are many others.

Some of these seminars and services, however, are only looking to make a quick buck out of your need. What you should do is research. Find out the answers to the following questions:
■ Who teaches?
■ What are their credentials?
■ Have they actually gotten paid for doing what they profess to know?
■ If it's a service, who else has taken the class?
■ Have they closed any deals?
■ Can they send you a list of their bona fides (the projects they've placed somewhere)?

Whenever researching someone, make sure you Google their name. Read reviews. Do a search for their name next to the word "fraud." If any links come up, they'll probably take you to a chat room where somebody has some kind of complaint against this guy or gal. Read through the thread. Learn to recognize a legitimate gripe, as opposed to simple meanness.

Agents and managers

The same goes for agents. Research who they are and whom they represent. An agent should never charge you any money up front. They only make money if you do. Ten percent is the customary amount, or fifteen for a manager.

Remember that the difference between a manager and an agent is that the manager will manage your career and make suggestions about what you should do next. They are more directly involved with your development. The agent is only there to field offers and negotiate contracts.

At the start you won't need an agent at all. In fact, getting one too soon, or getting the wrong agent altogether, can hinder your career. First, you need to gather experience. You don't need to get an agent to work on projects you won't be getting paid to do. Those are the types of projects you'll probably start out with. They'll offer meals and a copy of the work. To begin with you'll take them and be happy to be getting the credit. Eventually you'll outgrow that type of work. You'll know when that is.

At some point you'll need an agent to handle offers for you. But the agent won't happen till after you get some work on a legitimate show or you win some kind of award at a major festival. Then you'll be ready to move on to the next level. Be patient!

Festivals

Whenever you are looking for work, the best calling card is a fantastic film. Make sure the work is solid and the jobs will come to you. The festival circuit is a great way to showcase your work and get good exposure. One thing to keep in mind about the festivals is that they're not all the same; also, they can be expensive.

The best way to submit your film to the festivals is through one of the current websites that link you to all the different events worldwide. At the time of writing, the one that dominates is Withoutabox.com. The websites will have a calendar and a list of the festivals as they take place throughout the year. There are hundreds. You can read the guidelines of each one and submit your film—note that you'll have to create a profile for your film and upload a digital version of it.

The festivals cost about $40–$70 a pop to submit your work, so be selective. And that's not the only cost you'll incur. If you're accepted, you'll have to provide a copy of the film in the festival's preferred format. (This is skewing more and more toward high-resolution digital copies.) The festival will also want to see a poster, a press kit, a website, and behind-the-scenes footage. You'll have to pay to have those set up, unless you can do some of the work yourself.

There are some website-building apps that are quite easy to use. Of course, that sort of thing always looks better when done by somebody who's done it before. A good website should take a bit of time to build. It should look legit and be easy to navigate. Don't forget to make it accessible from both a computer and a mobile device. Make sure it's working properly and up to date.

If you get accepted, you'll want to attend the festival and enjoy the festivities. That can get costly, too. We're talking airfare, hotels, transportation. It's a good idea to start with festivals that are in cities you can easily travel to.

When you attend the festivals, go to the parties, talk to the other filmmakers, and generally mingle. That's the main appeal of the festivals anyway. The trend toward big deals at the festivals diminishes each year. In fact, there are only four festivals at which big deals happen: Sundance, Cannes, Tribeca, and Toronto. Some filmmakers will argue that those are the only ones that matter, but I disagree. There are lots of other great film festivals, such as Berlin, South by Southwest, LA International, and others.

If you get a chance to go, you'll meet like-minded individuals, and that's really useful, as you never know where your next collaboration will come from. That's why I suggest you go to the parties and network. Learn the skill of working a room. It's easy—you just walk up to somebody and ask them what they do. Ask them about their work and their lives. People love talking about themselves, so make it about them. Exchange cards. That's what the festivals are really good for.

When going to parties in a town where the industry is strong, like Los Angeles, always hang around, always work the room, and always bring business cards.

Climbing the ladder

You know you can't start out working as a PA and expect to climb straight up the ranks to become a director. It just doesn't work that way. Nevertheless, at some point you're going to have to make the leap and start directing. And if you just graduated from film school, you should have the hardest commodity to come by in the film business: a crew.

As I've suggested previously, go out and shoot something. Start with shorts, because shooting a feature is a tricky business, needing a lot of stamina and know-how. An indie feature takes, on average, three to five weeks to shoot. That's a long time to be doing 12-hour days, which is why you want to start small, with a short. Several shorts, in fact. A feature would also require more money than you probably have at the moment. Your crew may be willing to work for you for free, but they will only do that for so long.

If you have a group of friends from film school, you can each shoot a short, and you can help each other. That'll help you work on your stamina for a future long shoot, and it'll also give you time to work on the script of the longer work.

You shoot your shorts. Then you take them on the festival circuit and hopefully you win some awards, or get noticed by some producer who's willing to work with you on your next project. Or at least you meet some more like-minded individuals with whom you can pool resources for the next thing.

When you're a filmmaker, you always have to be thinking about the next thing. One of my good friends from New York, who was the AD on the last short I shot there, is the hardest-working director I know. He goes from project to project, often without a break. I think he has two or three projects in development at all times. He finishes one, there's usually a previous one he's doing the rounds at festivals with, and he immediately starts something new. He's really a marvel of focus, talent, and dedication. Ultimately that's what you want to do. You don't want to stop working.

THE FEATURE

Eventually the time will come to shoot a feature. Here are a few things to keep in mind.

You're going to need money (see page 193). It's not impossible to do it without money but it nearly is. It's just a matter of the amount of time and effort it takes to coordinate all those people and resources for a prolonged time. If you have no money and if people are just doing you favors, then you'll have to wangle their schedules, piece by piece, which will probably leave you only able to work on the weekends.

That can be done but it's going to take twice as long, and the longer you're out there without finishing, the easier it is for something to go wrong and stop you from finishing at all. An actor may move away, you may lose a major location, you may no longer have access to your camera. Any number of things can derail you.

The best way of proceeding is to shoot the feature all at once. It'll take you at least two to three weeks, each consisting of six twelve-hour days.

The other reason you'll need money is that, by the time you're ready to do your feature, you'll need to start thinking about hiring some other artists to help you with the details of the film. Mainly you'll be thinking about a production designer, a hair and makeup person, and a costume designer. That's just for starters.

When you first begin making movies, you tend to do without these people because you're working with a skeleton crew. But as you gear up for your feature, you'll want to pay more and more attention to this kind of detail. It's not worth it if you don't. Having another artist whose job is to take care of just one aspect of the look of the film will do wonders for your end product. Production quality will go up tenfold—and you want this if you expect to make some waves with your feature.

GETTING THE FUNDING

The first thing you want to do is hook up with a producer who has some connections—somebody who's looking for material and hopefully has produced a feature before. The festivals are great places to find people like this. The other way is to impress with your script.

Work diligently on your screenplay and make sure it's ready before you start showing it around. I suggest you write at least three or four versions of it. Getting a second opinion is a good thing, so ask a couple of friends to read it and give you notes. Listen to their notes and take time to internalize them. Don't be too quick to trust your own opinions about your work—if two or more readers give the same note, then you should probably address that problem before a producer reads it.

Before you start showing it to people outside your immediate circle, you'll want to register with the Writers Guild of America (WGA). All you have to do is go to their website www.wga.org and click on the link that reads "register your work." You'll need a credit card to pay the registration fee, and the website will ask to browse your computer in order for you to upload a digital copy of the work. You don't need to be a member of the Guild in order to register your work.

register

The registry serves as proof that you wrote the script at the set time. If there were ever a dispute, then the registry would serve as your guarantee.

The WGA registry is not the copyrights office—that's the Library of Congress—but you don't really need to worry about the copyright just yet. If the movie gets made and perhaps a hard copy of the script is made available to the public, at that point you can apply for the copyright.

Once your script is registered with the WGA, you'll want to get it out there. There are contests, fellowships, and websites that promote scripts and that producers go to, to find material.

Almost every festival has a screenwriting contest attached. You find out about them through one of the websites that lists the festivals, such as Withoutabox.com.

Some of the contests offer fellowships and workshops. Here you'll be given the chance to workshop your script for a period of time with all expenses paid and a group of professionals to help you develop the piece. The two most notable ones are the Nicholl Fellowships in Screenwriting and the Sundance Screenwriters Lab.

Getting into these programs is a great thing. Keep in mind that the competition is fierce and your work needs to be top-notch.

There are websites that claim access to producers, and some of these are excellent. The most prominent one is The Black List, and it is rumored that some of the great unproduced scripts in Hollywood are there. Producers go to this website to search for material. The process for getting into The Black List is quite competitive.

Option agreements

Once you get a producer interested, then they're going to want you to sign an option agreement for your script. The option allows them the right to negotiate on behalf of the project. Without it, a producer will be reluctant to work with you, because they could be working on a deal and then in the middle of it you sell the script from under them, meaning that they've lost all the work that went into making the deal happen.

The option protects the producer from that. It is basically an agreement between you and the producer that says that the producer owns the rights to your script for a set period of time, with options to renew. That period of time is usually one year with an option built in to renew if both parties agree or if they're in the middle of a deal.

For this option the producer will pay you a price that goes into your payment for the rights if the script gets sold. If you're an unknown writer, the price is usually $1, which is, of course, just symbolic. If you're a known writer, then this price can go up considerably. Dan Brown made $6m for the rights to *The DaVinci Code*.

payment

Where to look

Once the producer has acquired the rights to your script, then they'll go about the business of trying to raise money for the project or selling it to a company that can. There are three basic avenues to raise money for a film: studios, independent investors, and private money.

Studios

These are the only ones that can really finance huge productions. In order to get financing from the studios, you'll need a way in—probably a producer who has access to the executives, an agent who does, or a filmmaker who already has a deal to produce material for the studios. It's very hard to get in when you're on the outside. You shouldn't get your hopes up if this is your first script. Unless you win the Sundance Lab or the Nicholl Fellowships, it will be an uphill battle. And yet you never know. That's the thing about this business—crazy things do happen all the time.

Independent investors

The second way to raise money for your project is through independent investors. These are people who have money, who may or may not have invested in films previously, and who are looking to get into the business. A good producer with this sort of connection is invaluable.

Private money

The third option is private money. Your uncle dies and leaves you some dough or you raise the money through crowdfunding. Of course, the budgets differ dramatically for each option, especially if you're going to try to raise the money yourself.

The producer who optioned your script will probably do a budget for the film, or they may hire somebody to do it. Once the budget is made, then you'll have a better idea of the amounts you'll need and how long it will take you to shoot. Actually, I should say how long you'll have to shoot. It's not about what you think it'll take—it's about how long the money will last. That's always the case.

Making the deal sweeter

The producer is going to want to make the deal as attractive as possible for investors or for the studios. In order to do this, they'll try to leverage assets in order to engender interest. The four major assets a producer will work with are the actors, director, demographics, and source material.

Actors

First and foremost are the actors, and this means recognizable names. The producer will try to get names attached to your project. The more recognizable a name is, the more advantage can be leveraged from it.

investors

You already know that actors are the most important commodities in the movie business, movie stars being at the top of the heap.

When a producer is trying to get an actor to commit to your project, they'll try to get a **letter of intent** from them. This means the actor signs a letter that says they're interested. Then the producer goes to the studios and says, "Look, Brad Pitt wants to do our film. Give us some money." The letter of intent, however, is not a binding contract. Actors can back out at any moment, and they do. That's why the average development time for a project in Hollywood is seven years. People come in and then go out. Things appear to be about to come together and then your star gets cast on another project and you have to find somebody else.

Director

The second asset that producers will leverage is the director. If the movie's being directed by someone with a track record of success, then that's a good thing for the studios. Think about it: Would you give a million dollars to somebody to direct a movie if they've never done it before? In the case of your project, let's assume that the director is you, and that this is your first, so unfortunately you're no asset at all. As a matter of fact, movie stars will avoid working with a first-time director. They know it could lead to all sorts of nightmares on set. So you'll actually be a liability.

studios

Of course, if you've had an award-winning short at a prominent festival, or you've directed a music video that has climbed up the charts, then that'll help the producer sell you as an asset.

However, the director is infinitely less important as an asset than the actors. Nobody really cares who directed the movie except maybe people in the industry and film students. The general public cares about who's in it, not who was making the decisions behind the scenes. There are some exceptions such as prominent directors like Quentin Tarantino, Steven Spielberg, and the like, but the power of the actors is still the driving force for multiplex audiences.

Demographics

The next thing the producer is looking to leverage is the demographics—in other words, who's going to be interested in watching this film. The bigger the demographics, the more attractive the material becomes.

One of the biggest demographic groups for the movies is teenage girls. They go to the movies en masse, multiple times, and they buy merchandise associated with the film. This is gold to the studios.

Be aware that there are some emerging markets in the United States and abroad. The fastest-growing demographic in the US is Latinos. In some states the growth is 200 percent or more, corresponding to the increase in highly educated and upwardly mobile young men and women. This is a new and emerging market that's now looking to consume high-quality items, including entertainment. It is directly reflected by the great number of shows, movies, and music geared up for this demographic. All you have to do is put on Netflix to realize how many new shows in Spanish are out there, and how many Latino-themed offerings are being created every day.

On the other side of the world, China is the great sleeping dragon. With restrictions being listed and deals being brokered every day, producers are falling over each other to have a chance to sell to that market. It's the sheer power of the numbers. Companies that didn't want to deal with the restrictions, like Google, now are singing a different tune. They realize that if they don't do it, their competitors will, and this is something they simply can't afford.

Hollywood is working hard to crack the China code and invade the market. The going is slow because restrictions are tough, and they change almost every day. This makes it difficult for the studios and the Chinese authorities to reach agreements about what's allowed to be in the film or not. But soon enough we'll have new markets opening up all over Asia. In the meantime, investors are looking to south of the border, such as Mexico, Brazil, and Argentina.

Source material
The other asset producers are looking to leverage is the source material. Does it have legs? Does it have a following?

If the material comes from a book that already has a following, that's a good thing. Trying to sell a script by an unknown writer is not the same as a best-selling book like *Fifty Shades of Gray*. One of them clearly has a big-time, built-in audience and a better chance of doing well at the box office.

The genre is a factor as well. Horror movies and action movies are some of the more bankable genres. They're good investments, because they tend to make money across some of the largest demographics and across international markets. It makes sense. People love to be scared, amazed, and thrilled. Also, because there tends to be less dialogue in these films, language barriers are no so much of an issue.

source

The teaser

Sometimes the producer will ask you to shoot a teaser trailer in order to sell the project. You may want to do this yourself without having some producer tell you to. The teaser is basically a trailer for a movie that hasn't been made. You can shoot it like you would a short.

Make sure you write a script for the teaser itself. Don't go out with your feature script and just shoot scenes from it. A teaser is another animal altogether. What you're trying to do is make a montage that will explain what the movie's about, show your skill as a director, and get the viewer excited about what the movie could be.

You usually do the teaser with actors who are not the actors you're looking to cast in the feature version of the story. But you want to get the best actors and locations you can for the limited budget you'll have.

The purpose of the teaser is to sell the longer work, so don't get bogged down with long, dramatic scenes. What you want is variety. If you're working on something that involves action or special effects, you'll want to show a sample of what you can do. This won't be the fully fleshed-out special effects you'll do in the movie once you get your budget. But you'll want to choose something you can do well and that will showcase your talent.

DISTRIBUTION

Once you get the money to make your film, whether it's $100m (which is very unlikely on a first try) or $100k, you'll want to make the best movie you can. I advise you to concentrate on that—prepare thoroughly, be diligent about your work, and stay focused.

When the film is done, distribution is the next step. Sometimes you can secure it before you finish. Distribution companies these days get into the financing business. They'll help you finance your film in exchange for the rights to distribute the film once done.

They may acquire rights for an entire country or even a region, or sometimes just for a set of theaters in specific cities. It all depends on the type of movie you make and how wide the audience for it is.

If a company acquires the rights for your movie to play in, say, Japan, then all other markets are still open to you. The same goes for US distribution. You may get a deal for some states, or for a region, or nationally.

Asian and Latino international markets have become a very viable way for a movie to recoup its cost. Sometimes movies that don't do well in the US find an Asian market that likes them, and they make a killing.

It's also become increasingly popular for indie films to secure distribution in cities where this type of movie can find an audience, in particular New York and Los Angeles, and sometimes Miami and Chicago.

It's difficult for films to secure US national theatrical distribution unless they're coming out of the studio system. And even then it's only the high-yielding films, like superhero movies. Although that landscape continues to change year after year, it seems that theatrical distribution will continue to be limited to these blockbuster-type films, since they're the only ones that sufficient numbers of people seem to want to go to see in the theaters. So get ready for another ten variants of *Spiderman* and *Pirates of the Caribbean*.

Once in a while you'll see exceptions like *Crazy Rich Asians* or *My Big Fat Greek Wedding* but these are not the norm. What's more, those films didn't get that distribution right away—they started in smaller venues and moved on to national distribution later.

Smaller films, or any other type of film for that matter, will have to find their methods of distribution elsewhere. But do not despair. Here's the thing to remember about distribution: There's more than one way to skin a cat.

Streaming services and cable TV

Distribution avenues for the internet are Hollywood's new bread and butter. All the different streaming services—such as Netflix, Hulu, Amazon Prime, Apple—populate a landscape that changes from month to month, so keep your ear to the ground for the latest developments.
- There's the on-demand window, where companies may acquire a license to sell your movie through an on-demand service.
- After that there's a cable TV window for the movies to play on channels such as HBO, Showtime, or Cinemax.
- Finally, there's traditional network TV distribution, where your movie gets to play on a channel, probably on a Sunday afternoon.

This all depends, of course, on the type of movie you've made. The movie *Parenthood* may find a spot on ABC's Sunday lineup, but *The Texas Chainsaw Massacre* is another story altogether.

streaming

Each window represents a period of time in the life of the film:

- First, there's theatrical release for a couple of months.
- That's followed by pay-per-view, download to own, and digital rental services for a few months.
- Usually subscription video on demand or streaming services such as Netflix come next.
- Finally, there is cable and broadcast TV, extending to one or two years after the completion of the film.
- In the middle of all of the above, there's the DVD release. There's still some money to be made here, although that avenue is closing year upon year as subscription-based streaming services take over the market.

To sum up, avenues are varied, changing every year, and can keep making you money for as long as the movie plays on TV or other mediums. The life of a film can be long and fruitful. So, as always, if you concentrate on creating the best product you can, the distribution will come.

READ THE TRADES

The trades are the newspapers of the industry.
Hollywood Reporter and *Backstage* are the main ones,
though there are others, of course. These publications
list the deals that are being made, actors that have
switched agents, networks looking for material, and
everything else that's of interest to a young filmmaker.
They come in print and online versions.

You need to be in the know about what's going on
in the industry—ignorance is not an excuse. If the

producer you're working with tells you that your writing style would work very well for Aaron Sorkin's new show, the last thing you want to say is, "Aaron who?" Or, "What show?" And, yes, this sounds like a silly example, considering Aaron Sorkin is one of the best writer-producers in Hollywood today. Yet a large proportion of my students don't know who Aaron Sorkin is when they come to film school.

Please don't let this happen to you. Read your industry news. The other reason you should read the trades is that the deals made with the studios and other companies will be listed.

One day you'll read that producer Joe Schmoe has secured a three-picture deal with Lionsgate. And you happen to know Joe from film school. Well, what a coincidence. Do you think this is a good time to send Joe your script with a note describing how much you enjoyed working together in school?

GOOD INVESTMENTS
- Get yourself an **IMDb PRO subscription**. It'll allow you to create and update your profile. IMDb lists past, present, and future projects for people in the industry. It's an invaluable source for news, star-meter rankings, agents, production companies, and more. It's also a great research tool for anybody who wants to work with you, as you can look them up on IMDb.
- Invest in **professional screenwriting software**. Nothing screams "amateur filmmaker" more than a producer getting a script on a free writing app that's not compatible with what the producer uses. Use what the pros use: Final Draft.
- Invest in a **subscription for a high-end online video platform** like Vimeo or the upgrade for YouTube. There's work that you'll want to put online, and you'll need high-quality uploads.

TO REEL OR NOT TO REEL

Having a director's reel is certainly an asset if you're planning on becoming a hired gun and getting work shooting commercials, music videos, or any other type of work that requires you to be hired. This is usually not work you've developed yourself, but something you'll be brought in on. In those cases, you should have a reel that showcases as many skills as possible as a director.

- The reel should start with whatever you have that might be recognizable. If you've shot a commercial that people might recognize or done some work on a TV show, then that's the first thing you should have on it.
- Go on to showcase what you consider your strongest suit as a director. If you specialize in beautiful shots, action sequences, special effects, horror, or simple dramatic scenes with actors, that's what you want to show. Do you need to include entire scenes? Not at all.
- You can format the entire reel as a montage. If you wish, you can lower the music and show a part of a scene that's particularly compelling, but you should move on to more dynamic footage as quickly as you can. Anything with good production values will do—for example, if the sets are beautiful, or the sequence involves some kind of stunt, or you have a particularly long and complex shot. Flashy goes a long way in selling you as a director.
- Any scenes you have with recognizable actors also help. It brands you as a pro and a director who knows how to work with talent.
- The entire director's reel shouldn't be more than a couple of minutes long. Shorter is better. Make sure your contact information is there at the end.

CASE STUDY: *MOONLIGHT*

To help your film stand out, make it as personal as possible—a movie with a personal story connects with an audience. The 2016 film *Moonlight* is a great example. Director Barry Jenkins based it on the play *In Moonlight Black Boys Look Blue* by Tarell Alvin McCraney. Jenkins had written a number of scripts after the 2008 release of his first film, *Medicine for Melancholy*, but none were produced. He kept searching for material to make a "cinematic and personal" film. Eventually he met McCraney and their collaboration began. By drawing on the semiautobiographical accounts of the play and his own upbringing, Jenkins was able to craft a personal film that connected with a wide audience. The movie became the first film with an all-black cast and the first LGBTQ film to win the Oscar for Best Picture.

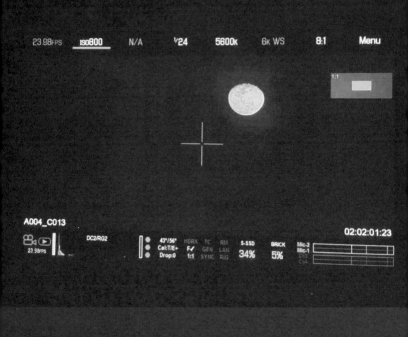

CONCLUSION

Be grateful for every day on a movie set. No matter how hard, it's better than a day in a cubicle.

When I was a kid I saw *Star Wars* 65 times. It sounds like an impossible number, but I'm sure there are people who have watched a movie more times than that.

When I did it, my mom had to go to the video store and rent the tape so I could watch it. It was the 1980s. The guy at the store knew her and knew who I was, even though he had never met me. At some point he gave her a terrible version of the film that had been dubbed into Spanish. Even the names of the robots were transliterated into Spanish. If you say C-3PO in Spanish, the last two letters, PO, mean "fart." It was hilarious because the name must be uttered hundreds of times in that script. All I could think about was that they were saying "C-three-fart, C-three-fart, C-three-fart."

When my mom took me to see *Jaws* for the first time, I was at a stage in my life where I carried a little cowboy gun with me wherever I went. It was one of those shiny ones that you fed paper caps into. The gun used to come in a set with a belt, a hat, and a sheriff's badge.

Anyway, when the shark appeared during the final sequence, little old me got up in the middle of the aisle and shot the shark dead, "Bang, bang, bang!" My mom hastened to sit me back down and shut me up. The people around us burst into laughter.

During one of the James Bond movies, I think it was *Moonraker*, I got scared of the man with the silver teeth and my mom had to take me out of the theater. For one of my birthdays, my parents bought our first videotape player. It was a Betamax. The first movie they got was *Raiders of the Lost Ark*. Or it might have been *Superman*—I can't remember.

What I do remember is the awesome power of being able to watch my fantasies whenever I wanted. To this day, I'm the type of person who watches movies multiple times to relive the moments I already know are there.

Sometimes when I'm with a friend trying to figure out what we want to watch on Netflix, they'll mention titles and I'll say, "Let's watch that one." They'll reply, "But you've seen it. Let's find something you haven't seen."

What they don't get is that watching something I've seen before, if I like it, is as enjoyable, sometimes more enjoyable, as gambling on something that I don't know is going to be any good.

Anyway, getting back to *Star Wars*, I watched it multiple times for the same reasons everybody else did. It had adventure and fighting, heroes and villains. But for me the character that sparked the greatest interest was Obi-Wan Kenobi. For some reason the image of the wise master always appealed to me in some deeper way.

As a kid, the show *Kung Fu* also made a great impression on me. The character of Master Po was fascinating. I've always wanted to be the aged master, still capable of kicking ass, but above the emotional attachment.

This book is a childish attempt at fulfilling that fantasy.

There's a video on the internet, with a voiceover by Alan Watts about dedicating yourself to doing something. In that way you can get really good at it, and then that's how you can demand to be paid whatever it is that you want to be paid for it. That's absolutely right. There are a few things in my

fantasies

life that I've been doing forever. Being involved in the arts, especially acting and filmmaking, is one. Teaching has become another. I really hope I come across as the aged Jedi Knight. In my eyes I'm still a Padawan learner but, like anything in life, how we see ourselves is not necessarily the impression we make on others.

Filmmaking, like any true art, is something you can do for the rest of your life. The levels of mastery and depth are infinite. There will be things about it that I'll still be figuring out on my deathbed. And as I lie there almost ready to check out, I'll say to myself, "So that's what that's all about!"

I'm ready and willing.

As I've said, being an artist requires a lifelong commitment. So I'll ask the questions I ask all my students when they invariably want to know whether they should be doing this or not. I say, "Are you going to go work at a bank? Be a lawyer? Study engineering?" They answer no. Then I say, "If you fail a few times, are you going to quit?" They also say no. "Are you ready to do this for the rest of your life?" They answer yes. "Then don't worry about any of that. Worry about keeping those answers true. And enjoy the process."

At some point in your life, somebody will tell you that you should do something more practical, that you should get your head out of the clouds. Or, even worse, they'll try to make you feel small because of

mastery

your choices, because you're in your 30s and you still can't pay your rent and they're running their father's business and have three kids and are successful.

They're the ones who took the easy road out. The world needs people like you who are willing to spend their lives in pursuit of a crazy dream.

I watched *Star Wars* all those times because that was my fantasy. Artists, be they filmmakers or writers or painters, don't discard those childhood dreams. We don't give up on them. We turn them into movies, or books, or other forms of expression. In doing so, we do it not only for ourselves, but for everybody else who's stuck in an office, in a world that has no wonder, no magic, no villains, no heroes, no wise old masters. We need to exist to provide them with what they crave, to feed that child inside, to remind them that the spark of life is not in making money or amassing possessions but in turning dreams into living works of art. That's the stuff we go to bed thinking about. That is the divine inside.

So go out there and do your best. In the immortal words of luminary George Lucas, by way of Obi-Wan Kenobi, "Use the Force, Luke…Stretch out with your feelings!"

enjoy

On Writing

On Writing: 10th Anniversary Edition: A Memoir of the Craft
Stephen King

Story: Substance, Structure, Style, and the Principles of Screenwriting
Robert McKee

Dialogue: The Art of Verbal Action for the Page, Stage, and Screen
Robert McKee

Ernest Hemingway on Writing
Ernest Hemingway and Larry W. Phillips (ed.)

The War of Art: Break Through the Blocks and Win Your Inner Creative Battles
Steven Pressfield

The Elements of Style, Fourth Edition
William Strunk Jr. and E. B. White, et al.

On Filmmaking

The Visual Story: Creating the Visual Structure of Film, TV and Digital Media, Second Edition
Bruce Block

Cassavetes on Cassavetes
John Cassavetes and Ray Carney (ed.)

Werner Herzog: A Guide for the Perplexed: Conversations with Paul Cronin
Werner Herzog and Paul Cronin

Film Directing Shot by Shot: Visualizing from Concept to Screen (Michael Wiese Productions)
Steven D. Katz

In the Blink of an Eye: A Perspective on Film Editing, Second Edition
Walter Murch

Screen Language: From Film Writing to Film-making (Screen and Cinema)
Cherry Potter

On Acting

The Art of Acting
Stella Adler

A Practical Handbook for the Actor
Melissa Bruder, Lee Michael Cohn, Madeleine Olnek, Nathaniel Pollack, Robert Previto and Scott Zigler

Michael Caine: Acting in Film: An Actor's Take on Movie Making (The Applause Acting Series), Revised Expanded Edition
Michael Caine

On Directing
Harold Clurman

Sanford Meisner on Acting
Sanford Meisner and Dennis Longwell

Directing Actors: Creating Memorable Performances for Film and Television
Judith Weston